About the authors

Dominic Haydn-Davies is a senior lecturer in Physical Education at Roehampton University. Before joining the university, Dominic taught in schools across the whole primary-age phase and worked as a school sport coordinator and partnership development manager in a large school sport partnership.

Dominic's research interests are in Physical Literacy, Foundation Stage Physical Education and Inclusive Physical Education and he has presented at local, national and international conferences. Over the years, a range of his professional and research articles have been published and he has worked as a consultant and author on resources for afPE and Youth Sport Trust.

Emerick Kaitell is also a senior lecturer in Physical Education at Roehampton University as well as an experienced coach in variety of sports, including trampolining, athletics, rugby and football, working with young people aged 3–18 years. His earlier roles as a secondary Physical Education teacher and as a partnership development manager within a school sport partnership have lent him extensive experience of working with schools and community groups in London to further sporting links.

Emerick has previously contributed to UK Athletics' *Elevating Athletics* resource for secondary schools. His research interests are in Continuing Professional Development (CPD) and Communities of Practice.

association
Physic
Educati

cal Education:

urriculum

Dominic Haydn-Davies and Emerick Kaitell

ISBN: 978-1-905540-79-2

Authors:

Dominic Haydn-Davies

Emerick Kaitell

We extend our thanks and appreciation to the following:

Dr Jon Spence; Victoria Randall; Helen Douglas and Peter Davies for their comments; former colleagues for their energy when trying these ideas; Naomi Voice; Hannah Gibeon and Charlotte Brien for their contributions; all of the Primary Physical Education Specialists at Roehampton 2006/9 and 2007/10 for their interest, questions, debate and enthusiasm for the subject, particularly the Croydon girls; and our families, especially Fiona, Owen and Meredith, for their patience and support.

afPE appreciates the contributions through review made by:

afPE project lead officer: Sue Wilkinson

Coachwise editor: Abi Masha

Coachwise designer: Carl Heath

Photographs © Alan Edwards

Published on behalf of afPE by

Coachwise Business Solutions

Room 117
Bredon
University of Worcester
Henwick Grove
Worcester
WR2 6AJ
Tel: 01905-855 584
Fax: 01905-855 594

Building 25
London Road
Reading
RG1 5AQ
Tel: 0118-378 2440
Fax: 0118-378 2442
Email: enquiries@afpe.org.uk
Website: www.afpe.org.uk

Coachwise Business Solutions
Chelsea Close
Off Amberley Road, Armley
Leeds LS12 4HP
Tel: 0113-231 1310 Fax: 0113-231 9606
Email:
enquiries@coachwisesolutions.co.uk
Website: www.coachwisesolutions.co.uk

Contents

Introduction

"Obesity Epidemic – Sport Boosts Friendships – Youth Crime Wave – Olympic Success – School Standards Slip – Social Breakdown – New World Record – Drug Cheats – Size Zero – Virtual Friends – Exercise Keeps You Young – No-Ball-Games Culture!"

This book is written against the backdrop of increased interest from the media, parents and wider society, in Physical Education. These groups may not realise that it is, essentially, Physical Education they are talking about, but perhaps that is the issue that faces the subject. Physical Education is a misunderstood area of learning, much of which is built upon negative recollections of personal experience in school. It is not a surprise that Physical Education is misunderstood; it is not a simple subject and has strong links to developments in the fields of sport, health, social development, education and the general well-being and welfare of children and young people.

In the UK this interest has been supported by increased government funding. It also comes at a time when schools are being seen less as the sole determinants of education and educational outcomes, and more part of a system that can contribute to the development of children and young people. In what is termed a 'multi-agency approach' there is a whole range of professions and professionals who are attempting to break down logistical, historical and social barriers. It also means that there are many more people with vested interests in how children develop. The once dualistic partnership between parents and schools has expanded; some of these interests are complementary whereas others present more of a culture clash and can even be in opposition.

This book is about how those with an interest in developing the **physical education** of children and young people can do this effectively. Although written very much with school teachers in mind, it is also essential that others who work in this field, such as sports coaches, dance instructors, fitness and health professionals and sports development officers, can access this type of information. It may also include those from uniformed groups, extended schools managers, play leaders, parents and volunteers.

The decision has been made not to tie the ideas and principles in this book too closely to any country's current opportunities, initiatives or strategies. Although increased priority, focus and funding is welcomed, the principles within this book should be able to be adapted for any setting, regardless of involvement, access or funding streams. Physical Education and programmes beyond the curriculum will always be needed, but funding and strategies change. Many of the ideas come from the English educational system, which has its strengths and weaknesses, but this is purely down to the authors' experiences.

This book is not about what needs to be taught in Physical Education lessons and is not based on any particular curriculum model. This book focuses on learning beyond the curriculum, for example, the opportunities that arise when children and young people are not in Physical Education lessons. While frameworks need to be met, often statutorily, these change over time. There will be principles that remain constant; *Chapter One* explores some of these and sets out why these are important. There are many excellent textbooks about Physical Education lessons, some of which are referred to within the 'Further Reading' sections of each chapter. Most importantly for this book, though, is our firm belief that to ensure a developmentally appropriate programme of opportunities beyond the curriculum, the opportunities need to be based on the foundation the curriculum provides. The learning programme beyond the curriculum should be seen as an extension, enrichment or enhancement of curriculum Physical Education, rather than just an add-on.

We do not believe that we have all the answers. The book does not aim to give a set of hard-and-fast rules and activities that will ensure success. Instead, it aims to get those who will be involved in establishing and developing programmes to think about the right questions, so they can find the right answers for their needs. Ideas will need to be adapted to each setting and also to the children and young people within those settings. The ideas and principles within this book are based on research, good practice and, most importantly, experience, which includes years of getting things wrong. This means we can now help people to ask the right questions, set the right foundations, look in the right places and make the right partnerships. It is essential that programmes are developed for the right reasons.

Terminology

Most terms are defined within the chapters in which they appear. However some of the following terms appear throughout the text.

- **Children** refers to those within primary education, aged approximately 5–11 years old.

- **Young children** refers to those below the age of five.

- **Young people** refers to individuals within or around the secondary school system, aged between 11 and 18 years. When referring to general principles the term **children and young people** is used.

- **Practitioners** is the term chosen to describe the whole range of individuals who may work with children and young people in the area of Physical Education. They include teachers, coaches, parents, volunteers and many other groups. If a specific profession of this group is being referred to, it will be stated within the text.

- **Physical Education**, in most cases, is used as a catch-all term for the wide range of physical activities available, including sport, dance and many others. It may also be referred to as **physical activity**.

- **Curriculum** refers to the planned lessons during school hours (from approximately 9am to 3pm), mainly under the supervision and direction of qualified teachers.

- **Out-of-school hours** refers to the time between 8am and 6pm that is not covered within the curriculum. This is specifically made up of 'travel to school', 'before school', 'break time', 'lunchtime' and 'after school'. This is also known as out-of-hours learning, extended provision or extended programme.

- **Community time** is considered to be between 5pm and 9pm, although some opportunities may occur from 3pm.

- **Learning beyond the curriculum** is not limited by time, but is more a summary term of all opportunities that occur beyond the normal planned curriculum. This includes all aspects of extended provision plus additional opportunities that occur within curriculum time, but beyond the normal scope of provision. It is also referred to, on occasion, as an 'extension' or a 'programme'.

- **Learning community** is a term used to incorporate all those involved in the planning, development, delivery and evaluation of an extended Physical Education programme.

Chapter Contents

This book is divided into three sections and each is important in establishing an inclusive and creative programme beyond the curriculum. Some sections will be of greater importance at different stages in the process of developing a programme beyond the curriculum, although it is suggested that, on first use, all chapters are read in order. There is no harm in reviewing things that may have become forgotten over the years! As experience grows, specific sections may have more relevance to the aspect of a programme that is in focus and should relate to the development plan being created and worked towards.

- Define your values

- Engage your learning community

- Be aware of your barriers

- Plan for impact

- Extend your day

- Reach potential

- Make the most of everything

- Celebrate!

Section A: Chapters within this section aim to set the scene for why a programme promoting learning beyond the Physical Education curriculum should be linked to curriculum provision, and who may be involved in ensuring that this happens.

- *Chapter One* outlines the supposed benefits of Physical Education and considers the importance of links between the curriculum and extended programmes to ensure good practice in both.

- *Chapter Two* focuses on who can form a learning community that will be charged with design, delivery and evaluation of a programme.

Section B: Chapters within this section look at two important areas when designing a programme: the inclusion of all children and young people, and the management and evaluation of a programme.

- *Chapter Three* establishes how a programme can be developed to include all children and young people. It focuses on supporting a range of additional needs, including special education needs (SEN).

- *Chapter Four* sets out the process that should be engaged to ensure that programmes are effectively researched, planned, managed, monitored and evaluated.

Section C: In the four remaining chapters, different aspects of a programme are discussed. Practical examples are given, as well as key principles by which to develop inclusive, innovative and developmental programmes.

- *Chapter Five* deals with opportunities that can be developed before and after school, focusing predominantly on a 'club' environment.

- *Chapter Six* focuses on competitive activities, including inter-school sport and sports day.

- *Chapter Seven* explores the possibilities within the school day for opportunities that develop understanding about physical activity or give opportunity for learning and activity.

- *Chapter Eight* outlines some of the special opportunities that can be developed, including residential experiences and sports weeks.

Key Features

Each chapter includes a range of information, examples, case studies, key questions, activities and ideas. *References and Further Reading* sections and links to the CD-ROM resources are highlighted by the following icons:

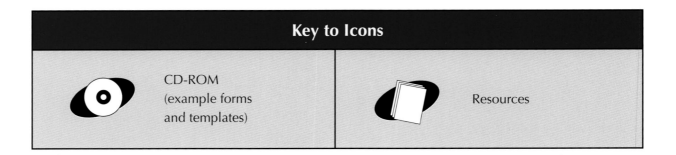

Key to Icons	
CD-ROM (example forms and templates)	Resources

Frequently Asked Questions (FAQs)

On pages 101–102 of this resource are lists of the FAQs from many colleagues over the years that became the catalyst to writing this book in an attempt to answer some of them. They are cross-referenced to pages within the resource that may provide useful information or points to consider.

Chapter one

Physical Education: Curriculum and Beyond

In this chapter you will find:

- a discussion about the benefits of Physical Education and why claims about its benefits should be realistic

- a brief summary of the relationship between Physical Education, health, sport and wider educational goals

- thoughts about why children and young people need Physical Education within **and** beyond the curriculum to successfully participate in physical activity throughout life.

1.0 Introduction

As stated in the general introduction to this book, the concept of Physical Education is often misunderstood. This chapter sets out to clarify reasons for Physical Education and the values it represents within education and wider society. It is proposed that a greater understanding of Physical Education can lead to a better understanding about why its curriculum provision (and that beyond it) is necessary.

The relationship between curriculum Physical Education and the learning beyond it is certainly not a case of the sum of two parts. There will be some who believe that both can coexist with limited links; the curriculum is for learning, whereas extracurricular opportunities are optional so their emphasis should be purely on fun. There will also be those who believe that the curriculum is not necessary if an extensive programme of additional opportunities is established.

This chapter aims to provide a strong justification for why opportunities that lie beyond curricular provision depend on quality provision within the school curriculum. While curriculum provision is often an entitlement, additional opportunities are, by definition, additional. There is an element of choice involved, but it is not as simple as merely a choice. Issues of access, information, understanding and support can all raise questions of equity of opportunity. If all children and young people are to receive the benefits of Physical Education, equality of access is essential and this is a major factor this book considers. Another is that for schools to promote the benefits of Physical Education, they first need to understand them and the implications of these benefits.

1.1 The Benefits of Physical Education

Physical Education, in all of its guises, sets out to engage children and young people in physical activity. It is widely acknowledged as being an important part of a healthy and positive lifestyle. A positive experience of physical activity at a young age should provide children and young people with the skills, attitude and motivation to continue to participate throughout their lives. It is therefore worrying that there is a significant number of children and adults for whom physical activity participation is not a regular part of their lives. It is also worrying that early experiences do not always seem to be positive predictors of future participation.

Physical Education in its widest sense is about more than just being active or taking exercise, or simply enjoying or getting better at sports. Physical Education in schools is often seen as existing to serve four areas of learning: health and fitness; sporting achievement; supporting academic learning; and developing social skills.

Assumptions, misconceptions and boasts?

While these four areas are commonly assumed as the purpose of Physical Education, evidence, research or practice do not always present a robust case to support these claims. The following sections look to explore some of these issues and implications. The *References and Further Reading* section will provide links to more expansive discussions on these topics.

Physical Education and health

The relationship between Physical Education and health promotion may sound obvious but this depends on how health is defined. There can be little doubt the school should have 'a potentially unrivalled position and privileged opportunity to make a better contribution to the health of future generations' (Waring et al, 2007). A broad interpretation of health, including all facets of wellness, physical and emotional health can be perceived as something education should aspire to contribute towards. Clearly, Physical Education also has a part to play in limiting negative health consequences, such as the current high-profile conditions of obesity and diabetes. The danger of this area of justification is that issues of health are extremely complex and if Physical Education claims to be the cure or prevention for a particular area of health, it becomes accountable for this outcome.

There is also the danger of limiting a view of health as merely being about size or weight (Evans et al, 2008). For example, obesity is a complex health issue, manifested in physical health matters, but bound with complex sociological and emotional issues. A few lessons of Physical Education each week is as likely to prevent obesity as it is to stop other types of illness. Wider health problems, encompassing physiological, medical and psychological issues are further possible outcomes of a diagnosis. What's more, ineffective Physical Education could also be suggested as one reason why people do not participate in activity, thereby having a potential negative effect on all-round health. Key messages need to be balanced and factually correct, not based on opinion, bias or myth.

physical education: beyond the curriculum

Current guidelines suggest a minimum of one hour of physical activity per day, for children aged 5–18 years (National Institute for Health and Clinical Excellence, 2009). Just as health is more than just being a 'normal' weight, Physical Education is more than merely running about or being active. Education is suggested to be the key to making informed choices about lifestyle and lifelong participation, so just being active is not enough. Recent guidelines (Association for Physical Education, 2008a) suggest that curriculum Physical Education should base around 50% of lesson time being active at an intensity that will contribute to health benefits. This provides a balance of activity for learning and learning for activity. A broad Physical Education curriculum cannot provide all this activity, which is why opportunities beyond the curriculum are required. Physical activity should be regular for it to become habitual but squeezing all of the emphasis into curriculum time could lead to it being something which is only done during that time.

Clearly, there is a significant and vital contributing role for Physical Education within health education, but it cannot be held responsible for children and young people's overall health. Therefore, it should not claim that it can be anything more than an important contributing factor.

Physical Education and sport

Physical Education and sport are not the same, although many common outcomes and shared activities demonstrate they are not entirely different. Common justifications for sport focus on the inherent opportunities to develop character, team skills and other aspects of social capital, while contributing to health and fitness. It is easy to see where sport can make these contributions, but there are also many cases where this does not happen. Consider the negative publicity sport receives in terms of morality, excess, lack of discipline, drugs, cheating, distorted body image and health complications. Is sport always a model that society should elevate for children and young people to aspire towards?

Whether participation in Physical Education can ever be linked effectively to sporting achievement and participation is a matter for discussion elsewhere, but a clear predictor would have to include the masses of children and young people who leave curricular Physical Education and never participate in any form of sport or physical activity again. Similarly, there will be those performing at the highest level who can clearly identify how little their Physical Education experiences contributed to their success.

There is an inseparable link between Physical Education and sport, but it is important that the two entities are seen as different, yet contributing towards many similar aims.

Physical Education and academic learning

The third common justification for Physical Education, particularly in schools, is that it helps children learn academically. Although there are lots of promising studies in this area, a conclusive and predictive link between physical activity participation and academic achievement has yet to be proved. A growing evidence base points to how exercise can positively affect brain performance (Ratey, 2009) but stops short of proving that intelligence can be increased by exercise alone. There is some common sense and many anecdotes to support the connection; the brain is part of the body and increased functioning may well be linked. However, there is also a huge number of very intelligent adults and children who are not physically active, and another huge number of physically active adults and children who struggle with learning and traditional aspects of formal education.

Certainly, Physical Education offers a myriad of opportunities for children and young people to develop key skills such as planning, communication, leadership, problem solving and thinking. However, it is only a vehicle for such learning, which can, and should, be developed across the curriculum. There is a significant amount of 'knowledge' to be learnt in the area of Physical Education, as attested by the increase in qualifications, examinations and degrees in this field, but just 'knowing' about the subject does not mean that children and young people will participate in youth or later life.

Physical Education and social skills

Within the activities, opportunities and experiences that Physical Education can offer there are many formal and informal prospects for children and young people to develop specific social skills, such as cooperation, communication, teamwork and responsibility. If opportunities are developed well and individuals supported effectively, this learning can certainly be promoted. However, if these skills are not taught, coached or supported, there are, equally, ample opportunities for children and young people to develop and enact antisocial skills like bullying, uncontrolled aggression, lack of respect and poor behaviour.

Thus, Physical Education can offer children and young people opportunity for excellent personal development. The four justifications described above can all be considered potential and desirable outcomes of Physical Education, but Physical Education needs to be justified for itself and its own worth. Reliance on any one of the four justifications over another can lead to conflict, as no single problem can be solved by Physical Education alone. It is not true to say that high level sporting performance is good for all aspects of wider health, just as being active for physical health benefits will not make you the best sports performer. It is much more complex than that.

A more cautious approach is promoted in a recent comprehensive academic review; Bailey et al (2008) conclude Physical Education can be beneficial if the approach meets the specific needs of the children and young people.

> The accumulation of evidence suggests that Physical Education and school sport can have some/many benefits for some/many pupils, given the right social, contextual and pedagogical circumstances.

This raises the need for more understanding in this area and the creation of a more evidence-based profession. The concluding comments of Green (2008) extend this debate further and other readings are suggested at the end of this chapter.

1.2 Problems with Physical Education

Physical Education is a part of school life that is a bit like Marmite: you either love it, hate it or just get it and put it in the cupboard, never to be used. Physical Education can make a valuable contribution to many aspects of children and young people's learning and all-round development, including those relating to health, citizenship and moral education. This breadth of purpose can also be seen as one of its weaknesses. A mixed message can be as confusing as no message at all and it is proposed that the main reason for problems within Physical Education stems from the value it is given by society, and more importantly, by schools. This lack of value comes back to a misunderstanding about the nature, aims and purposes of Physical Education. How importantly a topic is valued by society and schools determines key factors in its successful delivery. The amount of time allocated to Physical Education within the curriculum and teacher training, particularly for primary teachers, is a common problem (Haydn-Davies et al, 2007).

A lack of confidence or focus can lead to a multiple-tier system where children and young people are made to believe that physical activity is something that they can not do. Moreover, some will be made to feel that physical activity is something with which they do not need to engage. If the benefits of Physical Education are fully understood and valued more highly, then schools should be aiming to ensure all children and young people can progress as far as possible in this area. Focusing on the long-term goals associated with Physical Education can help provide some perspective with this, as it shows that schools cannot be held wholly responsible for the outcomes. Lifelong and life-wide participation needs support from a wide range of sources over an individual's lifespan (Penney and Jess, 2004).

1.3 Providing a Foundation for Lifelong Participation

For the purpose of this book, Physical Education is defined as involving 'learning to move and moving to learn' (Association for Physical Education, 2008b). This can be further expanded as involving education **about** movement, education **through** movement and education **in** movement (Arnold, 1979). The key aim of curriculum Physical Education has been articulated as to 'systematically develop physical competence so that children are able to move efficiently, effectively and safely, and understand what they are doing' (BAALPE et al, 2005). Physical Education, both within and beyond the curriculum, is one of the first, and arguably most inclusive, opportunities to develop an early positive experience of physical activity. It must also provide the fundamental foundations for future participation.

There are no set rules for what will make a child become an active adult, just as there is no single way of ensuring a talented youngster becomes a champion. There are too many other determinants involved for it to be that simple.

Research does, however, suggest key factors that may help in achieving the aims of Physical Education. If the aims are considered as developing physical competence, with an aspiration for children and young people to choose to be active throughout their lives, the following principles can give practitioners an idea of the needs of children in this area.

Ten key principles of practice within and beyond the curriculum

1. **Children and young people are all different**. Children and young people are not the same as adults; they all develop along a similar pathway, but at different rates, depending on a combination of nature, nurture, opportunity and support. Children and young people are all different in terms of their physical, social, emotional, cognitive and creative development. Age is a guide but not a set predictor of development.

2. There is a general set of physical skills that need to be mastered if children and young people are to be able to access different types of activities throughout their lives. Without these fundamental skills, children and young people are likely to meet a **'proficiency barrier'** (Seefeldt, 1980) that limits further progress.

3. Children and young people need three things to progress: **competence, a sense of autonomy and relatedness** (Deci and Ryan, 1985).

4. **Competence**, or mastery, **takes time**, effort, practice, repetition, support and reinforcement.

5. **Physical competence**, both perceived and actual, **can affect self-esteem** if what is being attempted is perceived as important by the individual. Given the messages currently promoted by education and wider society about the importance of healthy and active lifestyles, sporting ability and social capacity, children and young people are likely to see this area as important; therefore, competence is vital.

6. Children and young people **need to learn about effort, luck and ability**. Young children have difficulty in distinguishing between the concepts of ability and luck. They mainly believe that by trying harder they will do better. As children develop, this understanding develops to incorporate such factors as social comparison, norm referencing, capacity and task difficulty. However, until this develops, accurate comparison and goal-setting can be limited.

7. **Self-referenced learning** (eg the promotion of self-improvement) can motivate children and young people in learning and developing new skills, solving problems and making progress over time.

8. **Peer-referenced learning**, or a greater focus on comparative learning, can lead to a drive to win, but also a tendency to hide incompetency, which can lead to drop out.

9. The **focus of practice for lifelong physical activity** should be on promoting self-determined motivation and developing a programme and atmosphere of developmentally appropriate activities, choice and self-improvement.

10. The whole **learning community has an important role** to play in supporting children and young people, and in determining their approach to physical activity participation. This is driven by upbringing, socialisation and the focus of the context (Sarrazin and Famose, 1999). The learning community needs to work together, with a consistent message, to give the best possible support.

Extra Curricula

1.4 The Importance of Learning Beyond the Curriculum

To achieve the broad aims of Physical Education it is essential that the curriculum is not seen as the only aspect of provision. A programme of learning beyond the curriculum can build on these foundations to support all children and young people in achieving their potential. This book is written in the belief that for this combination of programmes to work, a common approach is needed in terms of opportunity, progression and philosophy.

For some children and young people, time beyond the conventional school curriculum has often been well utilised for physical activity, either formally (such as clubs and competitions) or informally (playtime and 'kick-abouts'). These opportunities are often labelled as being separate to Physical Education – sport, school sport, play, 'rec', leisure, extracurricular – to name a few examples. Where they are seen as separate, it is possible that different sets of aims and values are applied. The principles suggested above are written with reference to children and young people, rather than to context or programme. They should be consistently applied across both curriculum provision and beyond.

Although consistency of approach is advocated, the differences also need to be acknowledged. Opportunities beyond the curriculum are different to the curriculum; they give chances to enhance, enrich and extend those 'core' learning experiences that are available within the curriculum. Participation in these opportunities is mainly by choice, although these may not be informed choices. Children and young people need support, encouragement and motivation to attend and they need to be able to see clearly how opportunities will link to their prior learning and help them improve. Children and young people also need to understand why additional opportunities are necessary.

A key factor in lifelong physical activity participation is that it becomes part of everyday life; it becomes habitual. Curriculum Physical Education refers to a set time in a school week when Physical Education occurs, but this time is limited. During the hours of 9am to approximately 3pm, the school curriculum time makes up only 21% of the day. It is likely, even in the most forward-thinking school or curriculum, Physical Education will only account for a fraction of this time. Two 60-minute lessons per week are only 8% of curriculum time. The number of days that children and young people are actually in school makes up around 50% of the year when weekends and holidays are included in calculations. This leaves a two-fold problem. Firstly, within a child or young person's life, the school curriculum directly accounts for only 11% of the time in a year. Secondly, within this percentage, Physical Education must balance its case with the wider needs of the child or young person, which includes such important skills as reading, writing, mathematics, computer skills, the arts, music, design, science and humanities.

There is also a range of barriers to participation (see *Chapter Three*) that can limit learning within curriculum time and beyond. Children and young people will need different amounts and levels of opportunities in order to reach their full potential. If Physical Education is so broad, how will there ever be any consensus as to an appropriate way forward? Seeing Physical Education as an ongoing journey across curriculum provision and beyond it, goes some way to giving the scope and time needed to develop mastery and motivation for participation. There also needs to be an understanding of some of the key principles of development within this area.

1.5 Conclusion

If the curriculum provides the foundation for learning, opportunities beyond the curriculum are required to enable this learning to become mastered and habitual. The curriculum needs to drive opportunities beyond its boundaries so that the experiences children and young people are offered have a consistent message regarding the development of physical competence. It does not need to respond to every opportunity that arises, but react to those that will enhance opportunities within the broad framework and ethos it has built. When new opportunities arise they should be analysed to see how they will contribute to the whole programme rather than just making a difference for a few weeks, or to reach a particular target.

Clearly, this is an important job that needs to be fulfilled, but not one to be achieved by a committed, enthusiastic and idealistic reader alone. *Chapter Two* sets out who you will need to work with to make this more of a reality and how you can engage them in the process.

Key questions

- What value is placed on learning within and beyond the Physical Education curriculum in your school?

- What links are there between curriculum provision and extended provision in your school?

- How well do you think key groups in your school understand the nature and purposes of Physical Education in the curriculum and beyond?

References and further reading

References

Arnold, P. J. (1979) *Meaning in Movement, Sport and Physical Education*. London: Heinemann Educational Publishers. ISBN: 978-0-435800-33-8.

Association for Physical Education (2008a) 'Health Position Paper: Physical Education and its contribution to public health', *Physical Education Matters*, 3 (2): 8–12.

Association for Physical Education (2008b) 'Manifesto for a World-class System for Physical Education', *Physical Education Matters*, 3 (4): 31–32.

BAALPE et al (2005) 'Declaration from the National Summit for Physical Education: London, 24 January 2005', www.afpe.org.uk/public/downloads/national_summit.pdf

Bailey, R. et al (2008) 'The Educational Benefits Claimed for Physical Education and School Sport: An Academic Review'. *Research Papers in Education*, 24 (1): 1–27.

Deci, E. L. and Ryan, R.N. (1985) *Intrinsic Motivation and Self-determination in Human Behavior*. London: Plenum Press. ISBN: 978-0-306420-22-1.

Evans, J. et al (2008) 'Health Education or Weight Management in Schools?', *Physical Education Matters*, 3 (1): 28–32

Green, K. (2008) *Understanding Physical Education*. London: Sage Ltd. ISBN: 978-1-412921-13-8.

Haydn-Davies, D. et al (2007) 'The Challenges and Potential within Primary Physical Education', *Physical Education Matters*, 2 (1): 12–15.

National Institute for Health and Clinical Excellence (2009) 'Promoting activity, active play and sport for pre-school and school-age children in family, pre-school, school and community settings', www.nice.org.uk/PH17

Penney, D. and Jess, M. (2004) 'Physical Education and Physically Active Lives: A Lifelong Approach to Curriculum Development', *Sport, Education and Society*, 9 (2): 269–288.

Ratey, J. and Hagerman, E. (2009) *Spark! How Exercise Will Improve the Performance of Your Brain*, London: Quercus. ISBN: 978-1-847247-20-9.

Sarrazin, P. and Famose, J. P. (1999) 'Children's Goals and Motivation in Physical Education', in Auweele, Y. V. and Biddle, S. (eds) *Psychology for Physical Educators*. Leeds: Human Kinetics Europe Ltd. ISBN: 978-0-736062-40-4.

Seefeldt, V. (1980) 'Developmental motor patterns: implications for elementary school physical education', in Nadeau, C. et al (eds) *Psychology of motor behaviour and sport*. Champaign Il: Human Kinetics. ISBN: 978-0-931250-08-8.

Waring, M., Warburton, P. and Coy, M. (2007) 'Observation of Children's Physical Activity Levels in Primary School: Is the School an Ideal Setting for Meeting Government Activity Targets?', *European Physical Education Review*, 13 (1): 25–40.

Further reading

Physical Education in the curriculum

Bailey, R. (2001) *Teaching Physical Education: A Handbook for Primary and Secondary School Teachers*. Abingdon: Routledge. ISBN: 978-0-749434-46-5.

Doherty, J. and Brennan, P. (2008) *Physical Education and Development 3–11: A Guide for Teachers*. Abingdon: David Fulton Publishers. ISBN: 978-1-843124-56-6.

Pickup, I. et al (2008) *Learning to Teach Primary Physical Education*. Exeter: Learning Matters Ltd. ISBN: 978- 1-844451-42-5.

Developmental Physical Education

Gallahue, D. L. and Ozmun, J. C. (2006) *Understanding Motor Development: Infants, Children, Adolescents, Adults*. London: McGraw-Hill Higher Education Publishers. ISBN: 978- 0-071244-44-2.

Pickup, I. and Price, L. (2007) *Teaching Physical Education in the Primary School: A Developmental Approach*. London: Continuum International Publishing Group. ISBN: 978-0-826487-60-5.

Problems in Physical Education – aims and values

Green, K. (2004) 'Physical Education, lifelong participation and "the couch potato society"', *Physical Education and Sport Pedagogy*, 9 (1): 73–85.

Griggs, G. (2007b) 'Physical Education: Primary Matters, Secondary Importance', *Education 3–13: International Journal of Primary, Elementary and Early Years Education*. 35 (1): 59–69.

Kay, W. (2002) 'Physical Education R.I.P?', *British Journal of Teaching Physical Education*, 34 (4): 6–10.

Kirk, D. (2005) 'Physical Education, Youth sport and lifelong participation: the importance of the early learning experiences', *European Physical Education Review*, 11 (3): 239–255.

McNamee, M. (2005) 'The Nature and Values of Physical Education', in Green, K. and Hardman, K. (eds) *Physical Education: Essential Issues*. London: Sage Publications Ltd. ISBN: 978-1-761944-98-0.

Whitehead, M. E. (2000) 'Aims as an issue in physical education', in Capel, S. and Piotrowski, S. (eds) *Issues in Physical Education*. London: Routledge. ISBN: 978-0761944-98-0.

Physical Education and Sport

Kirk, D. and Gorely, T. (2000) 'Challenging Thinking About the Relationship Between School Physical Education and Sport Performance', *European Physical Education Review*, 6 (2): 119–134.

Lee, M. J. (2003) 'Values in Physical Education and Sport: a conflict of interests?' *British Journal of Teaching Physical Education*, 35 (1): 6–10.

Murdoch, E. B. (1990) 'Physical Education and Sport: The Interface', in Armstrong, N. (ed) *New Directions in Physical Education*. London: Continuum International Publishing Group. ISBN: 978-0-304334-49-9.

Psychology of Physical Education

Auweele, Y. V. and Biddle, S. (eds) *Psychology for Physical Educators*. Leeds: Human Kinetics Europe Ltd. ISBN: 978-0-736062-40-4.

Chapter two
Establishing an Effective Learning Community

2

In this chapter you will find:

• ways to identify the potential learning community in your school

• examples of how you can find, keep and develop key personnel in your learning community

• key information that you need to know about your learning community and what they need to know about your school.

2.0 Introduction

The term 'learning community' means many things within education. It can focus on schools reaching out into the community, or the community supporting schools by working with or within them. It can also mean a whole range of individuals working and learning together. This collaborative nature is required to ensure the links between children, young people, the school and community are effective and commitment is shared. Within a learning community, Rogoff et al (2002) suggest that 'learning activities are planned by children as well as adults…parents and teachers not only foster children's learning but also learn from their involvement with the children'. This chapter will investigate how the use of the community within and beyond the school can assist in reaching targets associated with Physical Education.

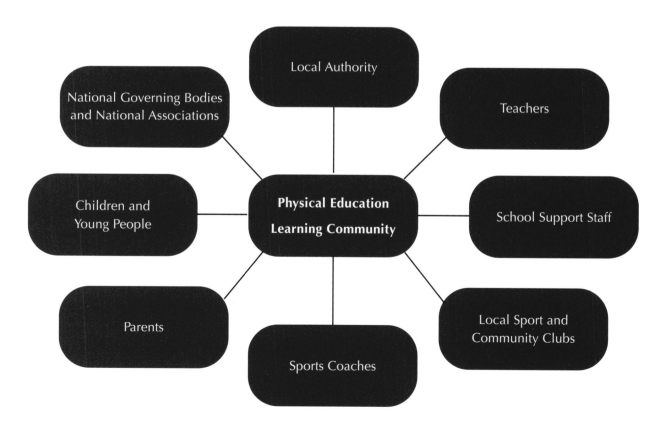

Figure 1: Potential members of the Physical Education learning community

Figure 1 illustrates some of the different sections of society that can potentially provide expertise and interests to support children and young people's development beyond the school curriculum. Individually, they can all have a modest impact on provision and development, but by working together they can establish a sustainable programme that changes and evolves to meet the ongoing needs of all within the school community. It is important for all parties to work together, combine their strengths and ensure a consistent approach. The opportunity to provide a comprehensive and consistent development programme can only be achieved through collaboration of all parties.

 ## Learning Community 5: Audit of Your Learning Community

Children and young people do not develop only within the curriculum and each of the groups mentioned above has to recognise its role in developing the new generation. The school must undertake a central role in organising the broader learning community to enable children to receive quality learning opportunities beyond the curriculum. Schools must provide strong and effective leadership by communicating their vision, purpose and principles. This can help the learning community to establish shared expectations, norms and a common direction.

The idea of developing this type of community allows all involved to develop a sense of group purpose and collective responsibility. A learning community relies upon clear communication and an understanding of the whole picture of children and young people's development to work effectively. Schools can benefit from engaging the support mechanisms beyond their boundaries to access expertise beyond their own abilities. Linking with these groups and utilising their expertise can improve the service provided for children.

The development of steering groups, committees or community support groups can give all parties a voice and provide a forum for establishing and communicating the ethos and aims of the programme, as well as providing opportunities for sharing recognition of each other's skills and expertise. It is of immense importance for the development of these opportunities that sports coaches, clubs, community groups, local authority staff and schools discuss and learn from one another to ensure coherent and effective programmes are offered to children and young people. It is essential that these interactions recognise the individual school's values and beliefs, and agree to its ethos and vision of purpose, so that all parties work together and the children receive a consistent message from all involved.

By working in this way, the quality of the provision, experiences and resources for children and young people can be enhanced. Although each member of the learning community will have different strengths, some assumptions can be made as to the impact of their contribution; for example, teachers are likely to have specific knowledge of working with and educating children and young people. Also, teachers, as well as parents, spend a lot of time with children and young people and may know them very well in terms of their ability and temperament. Similarly, coaches and external providers are more likely to have a better technical knowledge of prescribed activities, so the fusion of these two groups will greatly improve the experience for the children, teachers and coaches. If each party investigates their own gaps in knowledge and receives support from experts to compensate for these limitations, they will develop and subsequently improve the service offered to children and young people.

Schools are important in supporting the communication process between external providers and those within the school environment, and this level of support needs to be established at the beginning of any learning community relationship. Induction of any external practitioner to the school ethos and environment is essential; one group for whom this has begun to become common practice is sports coaches. The methods for induction will vary; however, the key principles, which are transferable for other practitioners within the learning community, are detailed below. Sports coaches are used to exemplify this relationship as they are some of the more prevalent and specialised members of a learning community.

2.1 Recruiting Members to the Learning Community

An Example: Sports Coaches

Although sports coaches are used as an example here, the principles relating to their recruitment and retention will apply to all members of the learning community.

Sports coaches can aid community learning by supporting physical activity during curriculum time or out-of-school-hours provision. Prior to engaging a coach, you should firstly consider these issues:

- target group – who is the opportunity for?

- aim – what are you trying to achieve for the group?

- choice of activity – what best suits the school's plans and ethos?

- role models – who will be most suitable to provide the opportunity?

- details – when and where will be most appropriate?

Understanding these issues will assist in identifying the most suitable sports coaches to meet the needs of the children, young people and the school. There are many definitions of a good sports coach and, in terms of best practice, the following criteria should be considered:

- expertise in the range of activities to be taught, ie:

    - technical knowledge

    - knowledge of progression

    - awareness of safety and accident issues

    - knowledge and application of rules

- knowledge of the group – their abilities, confidence and particular needs

- familiarity with the aspects of learning within any prescribed curriculum process model

- the observation and analytical skills to ensure that what is going on is safe and to amend anything that is deemed unsafe

- effective class control.

(Whitlam and Beaumont, 2008)

 Learning Community 6: Expression of Interest

Finding and keeping good coaches

Finding sports coaches is a very straightforward task, but finding good coaches and keeping them is another, more complex one. One of the key aspects of maintaining a good relationship is valuing the practitioner, who needs to gain something other than employment from being involved in the learning community. There must be clear and open communication concerning the expectations of the relationship from the outset, so that all parties understand their commitments. Sports coaches should be informed of how they can successfully meet these requirements. A formal induction process can help to clarify these matters.

If a school is looking to engage a high-quality coach they should consider what they can offer the coach. They will need to know:

- where this opportunity fits within the school development plan

- the funding stream that will be utilised

- what their coach induction process involves

- how the school will help the coach to develop

- how and when the process will be reviewed.

The above points link with the establishment of a communication channel between school and sports coach. Engaging sports coaches' views and opinions will lead to an improved understanding of the school's plans for the children and young people, and valuing the coach can lead to building a loyal relationship. If sports coaches are inducted into the school and feel they are part of the school, they will complement and contribute to the school community. They need this connection to ensure they are delivering appropriate programmes for the school; without it, there is the possibility the coach will not meet the school's needs.

The following sections will outline some of the general expectations for sports coaches and schools. For more detailed and thorough guidance, support should be accessed through local authority channels or via the sources in the *References and Further Reading* section of this chapter.

2.2 Information about Practitioners

Qualifications

Minimum qualifications for sports coaches are linked to national governing body qualifications. In the UK, the minimum standard that should be met is Level One, which relates, in many cases, to being an assistant coach. A higher-level qualification is desirable for employers, and may be essential for specific opportunities or for more substantive posts.

Sports coaching certificates will relate to a specific sport; however, there may also be the need for further qualifications if a specific group has particular needs. More able performers may require a more qualified coach, but that is not to say that those who are less able would not also benefit from this increased level of expertise. Within most sports and physical activities there are often additional qualifications associated with working with special groups, such as young children or children and young people with disabilities. If opportunities are targeted in this way, these extra qualifications may prove useful.

Regardless of qualification, new practitioners should be observed and supported where necessary to ensure the skills expected from the qualifications are being fully utilised. In addition, the wider education of the sports coach may be reviewed, including whether they have attended courses relating to Physical Education curriculum provision and, specifically, working with children.

Experience

Qualifications are one benchmark to check, but cannot provide the whole picture as to the suitability of the coach. Questions should also be asked of the sports coach in relation to his or her experience of the specific target group. A sports coach may have high qualifications and years of experience, but may have worked only with adults. On the other hand, a sports coach with limited qualifications may have always worked with children. Who would you want to work with your children? As with any employee, certificates should be copied for school records and references should be taken up and recorded appropriately to help evidence experience.

Schools need to consider whether they are willing to give less experienced coaches a chance to develop within a supportive environment. If this can be achieved while ensuring quality for the children and young people, it may prove a more cost-effective and sustainable model.

Other information

Another essential factor involves obtaining the following certification:

- A **Criminal Records Bureau** certificate is the first documentation that is needed. It demonstrates that appropriate checks have been put in place to ensure the coach is suitable to work with children and young people. This check highlights any criminal convictions on which the school can make a decision about the applicant's suitability for employment. Clearly, this needs to be dealt with confidentially and with discretion. There are certain convictions that would be entirely inappropriate to consider as acceptable, but scrutiny needs to be relevant to the nature of the employment, level of supervision and access to children and young people.

- **First-aid qualifications** may be needed if the school is not providing support in this way. Often, there is a named first-aider on the school site during the time of the opportunity, but such arrangements need to be explicitly agreed and confirmed with all parties. In most cases, higher-level coaching qualifications will be awarded only if the individual has a current first-aid qualification.

- **Child protection course** attendance is also promoted as good practice as this shows the coach's understanding of important issues relating to the children and young people with whom they are working. Many sport-specific courses cover techniques and sport-specific information, but do not cover child protection procedures. A coach who is aware of these issues is more likely to be able to meet the needs of all children and young people.

- **Insurance** is often covered as part of a professional qualification or through schools' policies, and it is vital that this is checked for every specific opportunity being developed. It should not be assumed by either party that insurance is being dealt with by the other. It is important that all parties are protected by insurance and, essentially, for the practices in which they engage.

 Learning Community 2: Sports Coach Application Form

As mentioned earlier, references from previous work with children can help to demonstrate a prospective coach's abilities and qualifications. Furthermore, they can ensure that coaches are suitable for the role within the school. Matching the strengths of the coach to the school requirements would help to develop improved learning opportunities for the children and young people.

The coach should complete an application form that includes:

- name

- address

- contact details

- qualifications

- personal information about health and disabilities (where appropriate)

- emergency contact details

- rationale for sport coaching

- previous work experience, paid or voluntary.

This information will ensure the school holds relevant information on all coaches and external support staff in case of emergencies, and illustrate that appropriate procedures have been followed. Action should also be taken to ensure that all payments are dealt with in the most appropriate way, in terms of taxation and other deductions. Local Authorities can help with these financial matters.

2.3 Information for Practitioners

Just as it is important for schools to know about coaches, it is also important that coaches are informed about the school and the groups with whom they will be working. Communication of expectations is important and these should be discussed with the class teacher in order to plan an appropriate programme and ensure children receive consistent and quality opportunities. As with all new school staff, the sports coach will require information concerning:

- behaviour policy

- reward policy

- incident reporting

- Special Educational Needs (SEN) register

- prior learning experiences of individuals within the group

- expected learning experience for individuals in relation to the curriculum

- timings of the school day

- first-aid and emergency actions

- register.

All of these points lead to a comprehensive and united partnership between the school and coach, enabling the children to receive high-quality learning experiences.

 Learning Community 4: Induction Records

2.4 Locating the Learning Community

The task of locating suitable sports coaches may seem daunting; however, there are support networks available to assist you. Local authorities, leisure centres, youth and sport departments, and governing bodies of sport will have their own databases of sports coaches working within a given area that they recommend. Coaching agencies are another source for finding sports coaches, as is the Internet. It is advisable to evaluate them prior to employment via interview and written school application with references.

Locating local sport clubs could also lead to the identification of appropriate sports coaches and investigating the local community from within is advisable. Information could be collated from children and parents as to where they attend physical activity and sport sessions outside of school and this could be displayed on the school's central information board. Compiling the information on a weekly planner, highlighting the activity to its specific days with the names of children who attend, will encourage others to attend and builds links between the school and club.

Networking with other teachers from schools within the area is another avenue for gaining information. Listening to other teachers enables a review of sports coaches' performance in a similar environment. Furthermore, planning an extended programme with other schools could ensure the best coaches are used by more than one school.

All the suggestions above provide links in establishing an effective learning community and building up knowledge of the local area. A greater understanding of the local community will make the task of locating suitable sports coaches and other practitioners easier.

2.5 Working Together

It is important the whole learning community understands how working together can help to establish the whole programme. It is important there is a common cause and identity, a clear plan, and a sense of trust between all involved. Ownership of the plan and programme by the whole learning community can help to foster this 'team' ethos. However, despite a school following all the principles set out within this chapter, things may still go wrong and it is important that the whole learning community understands what happens if this occurs.

The school (essentially, the head teacher and governors) is ultimately responsible for activities during school time. Equipment and facilities used on the school site remain the responsibility of the school, unless specifically detailed within a contract or service level agreement. With regard to employing external practitioners, all parties need to understand where responsibilities lie so appropriate action can be taken. Risk assessments should be carried out by the school and external party together, so all aspects are covered and understood.

Where practice does not meet with expectations that have clearly been set out in agreements, there may be cause for complaint. Procedures should be established prior to engagement of work, so all involved are aware of roles and responsibilities. As with other employees, there are procedures for complaints and, if the coach is sourced from an external agency, the agency will need to be informed of these concerns to aid them in rectifying the issues. If the coach is independent then the assigned member of staff is to inform the coach of the issue and proceed with a plan of action.

Complaints must be recorded with a clear 'action taken' section to illustrate the complaint has been acted upon. This may be used as evidence in future to inform the coach of their performance. No complaint is minor and all issues should be investigated, as with any school staff complaint. Establishing this procedure will ensure the coach has the opportunity to rectify the matter and provide an improved service. This should also be the process if the coach feels they have a complaint in the way the school is dealing with them as an employee, contractor or volunteer. The concern is that when the school does not communicate effectively with the practitioner, the issue increases and becomes a larger problem. Therefore, clear systems should be in place so that the school can be open to honest and constructive feedback from the learning community on how the programme is working. *Chapter Four* focuses on other aspects of monitoring and evaluation that can also be useful.

Establishing an appropriate procedure of verbal and written warnings, followed by a final warning, should ensure the school has provided the coach with the opportunity to improve performance. It should be remembered that sports coaches talk to one another about experiences in schools and a school with clear guidelines will receive positive remarks.

As with employees, the highest standards of delivery should be expected that meet the needs of the school and, more importantly, the children and young people. A clear service level agreement or job description can help with clarifying expectations as practitioners or volunteers should also know and understand what they are undertaking. The school's quality assurance systems, through information gained from children, parents/carers and teachers, will provide evidence of performance. Ensuring the coach understands the purpose of the activity and the criteria for success will assist this aim. Most professions have set national standards, which may be relevant to include within role descriptions and may be of particular relevance if the relationship is long-term or for a significant amount of time, where training and development may be part of the relationship.

Sessions should be evaluated so improvements can be made where necessary. This also serves to demonstrate what has proved effective. Monitoring should be seen as the norm and part of regular practice, not as judgemental or 'spying'. If the learning community has a common purpose, with shared expectations, then monitoring becomes productive and positive, helping to improve the programme and personal practice and to develop the learning community as well as the children and young people.

 Ideas 2B: Example Risk Assessment

Learning Community 1: Service Level Agreement Between School and External Partner

Learning Community 3: Coach Assessment and Evaluation

2.6 Conclusion

Although much of this chapter has focused on sports coaches, the learning community is much wider than just this one profession. The practice promoted within this chapter should help all members of the learning community to establish the common purpose and make the practitioners feel wanted and valued by the whole school. Involvement should not be limited to delivery of sessions; there will be many parents and other people with skills in finance, administration, media work or research who may be willing to help. Some may want to be involved in terms of collecting fees, registering or designing newsletters. Others may be able to help in terms of supporting individual children or young people, mentoring specific performers or inducting other members of the learning community. Looking beyond delivery, there are many roles and responsibilities that require personnel to ensure that the school is delivering high-quality programmes.

Once the key vision is established and the learning community engaged, a programme beyond the curriculum can be developed. The following chapters set out important principles for ensuring these programmes can meet inclusive aims and are well managed and evaluated. Once these principles have been established, practical ideas can be put into action.

Key questions

- Who is missing from your learning community?

- Do you know enough about the people in the learning community?

- How will you encourage people to become part of your learning community?

 References and further reading

References

Rogoff, B. et al (2002) *Learning Together: Children and Adults in a School Community*. US: Oxford University Press. ISBN: 978-0-195160-31-4.

Whitlam, P. and Beaumont, G. (2008) *Safe Practice in Physical Education and School Sport*. Leeds: Coachwise Business Solutions. ISBN: 978-1-905540-54-9.

Further reading

Association for Physical Education and sports coach UK (2007) *Adults Supporting Learning (including Coaches and Volunteers): A framework for development*. Leeds: Coachwise Business Solutions. ISBN: 978-1-905540-28-0.

David, T. (1994) *Working Together for Young People: Multi-professionalism in Action*. London: Routledge. ISBN: 978-0-415092-48-7.

Wenger, E. (1998) *Communities of Practice: Learning, Meaning and Identity*. Cambridge: Cambridge University Press. ISBN: 978-0-521663-63-6.

Chapter three
Ensuring an Inclusive Programme

3

In this chapter you will find:

- some of the key barriers that limit physical activity participation for children and young people

- a brief rationale for why provision beyond the curriculum needs to become inclusive

- frameworks and ideas to help support a wide range of children and young people with additional needs.

3.0 Introduction

One of the key principles of curriculum design is that the curriculum should be inclusive of the individuals for whom it is designed. Establishing a programme of opportunities beyond the curriculum should not mean abandoning the good practice it identifies. A school curriculum and, by extension, programmes beyond it, should be accessible and enabling to all the children and young people for whom it is designed.

Historically, provision beyond the curriculum has focused on only the more able, those who 'can' (Penney and Harris, 1997; Green, 2000). Teams for competitions are chosen from largely the same small group of participants, with the same children and young people being picked first, regardless. They are the 'sporty ones' and may well be the best; being the best is one of the component parts of competition and in terms of Physical Education, this is known as realising potential. However, this does mean that there will always be some who are picked last. The established argument has been that children who are not considered talented or sporty will not want to make use of opportunities. This does not amount to saying that they can't, but more that they will have other interests. If they are not the 'sporty type', they are more likely musicians or artists, scientists or mathematicians. This assumption is based on presumptions that you can only be interested in one exclusive area in life and that physical activity participation is an 'either/or' pursuit, rather than the fluid and transient journey that it should be throughout life.

The problem, or rather the challenge, comes when you develop and establish an inclusive and quality curricular programme. This raises not only the abilities of the children and young people, but also their aspirations and expectations. Reflect back to *Chapter One* where it is suggested that if children and young people see something as important then success in that area becomes imperative for their overall self-esteem. If schools and society are promoting health and fitness or sporting prowess as valuable, they have a duty to enable all children to achieve this goal.

Opportunities beyond the curriculum are not necessarily limited in the same way as curricular provision, as they do not necessarily have to include all children and young people in the same learning experience at the same time. Curricular provision is often differentiated to include as many learners as possible, but this is no easy task given the range of abilities and needs within a group that can be in excess of 30 children and young people. Opportunities beyond the curriculum could be targeted more, so that the range or number within the group is fewer and more manageable.

Targeting provision and opportunities may not appear to be equitable, as each opportunity will exclude others. It is not expected that one child will access all of the opportunities provided, but it is important that each child can access something. This is why understanding the needs of each child and young person is so vital in planning the programme. The range of additional needs found in every school is extensive, with each child bringing their own unique talents and challenges to a situation.

> ## Reflective task
>
> Think about yourself for a moment. What impact do, or could, the following factors have on your participation in physical activity, with regard to your:
>
> - gender, race, religion, culture, level of education and any learning difficulties
> - ability to cope with pressure – your tenacity and emotional fortitude
> - energy levels and enthusiasm
> - language skills, sociability and communication skills
> - behaviour, response to risk and competitiveness
> - personal organisation
> - attachment of importance to physical activity
> - physical fitness and health
> - physical competence and perceived ability?
>
> (This list may be exhausting but is not exhaustive!)
>
> Can you carry out this task for one child or young person in your class? How about the whole class?
>
> Within one class or group, each individual will be just that, an individual. There is no 'normal' or 'usual' type. Each child or young person will, more than likely, fit into many different groups or identities at any given time. These will change over time, in different contexts and situations. The child or young person may also have different aspects of their personality that will either cause barriers to participation or act as a stimulus for participation.

3.1 Assumed Barriers

It is often presumed that certain groups of children and young people are less likely to participate in physical activity. These include teenage girls, children with physical disabilities or from specific cultural or ethnic groups, and those who are overweight. Although there is evidence supporting these views, to be truly inclusive, all children need to be considered. Targeting these stereotyped groups can help, but can also isolate, exclude or even mask other non-participants from within, supposedly, active groups. There are many girls who do enjoy lots of physical activities, such as dance, gymnastics and netball, with which society makes immediate and easy links. There are also many girls and young women who enjoy and excel in other activities, such as rugby, cricket and football, where their acceptance in these sports is still developing. Boys are expected to enjoy football and more physical activities, while avoiding dance and aesthetic activities, and it is sad to think how many boys have not reached their full physical potential because they were not encouraged to participate in these types of activities where they may have excelled and flourished. Times and views are changing, but slowly.

In relation to SEN, it is often those children and young people with physical or sensory needs who are assumed to have the most significant barriers to participation. However, often it can be those with social or emotional needs that cause the greatest disruption or reason for non-participation. These needs may include those relating to how children or young people interact with each other in terms of behaviour, language or social skills.

A study by Coates and Vickerman (2008) outlines some of the issues relating to the inclusion of children and young people in physical activity, focusing on the perspectives of the participants themselves and raising some important issues. Firstly, they identified that positive experiences stem from feelings of competence, social belonging and acceptance of the participant's ability. A welcoming environment and an involvement in decision-making were also highlighted. Although this study focused on one specific group of children and young people, surely these factors would also be considered best practice in terms of giving all children and young people a positive experience?

Similarly, negative experiences for the participants tended to be characterised by a feeling of social isolation; for example, having their competence questioned and adults making the assumption that they did not have the ability to participate fully. This was often exacerbated by the teacher's lack of experience in the area, discrimination by others, feelings of self-doubt, barriers to inclusion and lack of empowerment and consultation. Again, surely these factors could also lead to negative experiences for all children and young people?

3.2 Possible Barriers

There is an almost exhaustive number of ways that physical activity participation can be limited for children and young people. Some of the barriers stem from external factors, such as finance, family, environment or social factors; others will have a more internal cause, such as low self-esteem or physical barriers. Certain causes may lead to a similar barrier being faced by more than one participant, but it is limiting to think that a child with condition 'A' will face exactly the same barriers as another child with condition 'A'. An important step is to think about the individuals involved and consider how they find physical activity participation difficult, how they respond to this challenge and how they can be best supported, given the possibilities.

Reflective task

Think about some children or young people you have worked with who have had difficulties participating in physical activity. From the table below, identify which barriers proved to be the most significant to them. Which barriers were the most significant for you?

Table 1: Different types of additional needs

Physical Need	Social or Emotional Need
Fitness levels	Attention and listening
General coordination	Behaviour
Hearing impairment	Communication and language
Medical conditions	Creativity and imagination
Movement-skill competence	Developing independence
Physical conditions	Emotional responses
Visual impairment	Following instructions
	Organisation
	Social interaction
	Understanding

These are only some of the general areas where a child or young person may find difficulties. Factors such as family, finance, culture, gender and religion could easily be added to this list, but overcoming these barriers will certainly rely on engaging with the whole learning community to ensure inclusion.

Some barriers have specific expressions within different contexts. Take, for example, a common opportunity within schools. A local sports club, in partnership with the local authority, has employed sports coaches to work with schools to develop their after-school provision and build links to the community club settings.

This sounds an excellent opportunity, but the following examples show how the breadth of additional needs can cause some schools to turn opportunities down.

Timings

What? A special school was offered extensive coaching after school for their young people. They said no.

Why? Over 90% of the young people were transported into school from outside the area and the school's minibuses were held to a strict timetable.

Possible solutions: Could the coaches be used within the lunchtime period? This is strictly outside the curriculum but within the school day.

Expertise

What? Well-qualified and experienced coaches, working in a community club environment, ran a club within a school. The school felt that the coaching did not engage all of the children and sessions were disorganised, so the school ended the arrangement.

Why? The group contained several children with specific SEN, including autism, attention deficit hyperactivity disorder (ADHD) and visual impairment. The coach had no understanding of how these conditions would affect the group. The club's sessions were limited to 16 participants, whereas school clubs took up to 25 to encourage inclusion.

Possible solutions: Could the coaches work with teaching assistants, teachers or support staff in order to gain experience of dealing with a diverse group? Schools need to ensure that coaches are provided with information about the children and are told what strategies have proved effective within the curriculum.

Priorities

What? A secondary school established a series of curriculum-enhancement sessions within an afternoon 'options' session. Young people from a particular cultural group did not attend any of the physical activity sessions even though the sessions included targeted activities that the children reported they had enjoyed within the curriculum.

Why? The session ran at the same time as other enrichment sessions that focused on more culturally valued skills, such as information technology and science. These particular young people felt pressured to choose and opted for those sessions they felt would enhance their employability.

Possible solutions: Could sessions be staggered or at alternate times? Could physical activity sessions be planned to promote skills and attributes that support wider learning areas, such as computer analysis? Could more be done to educate the wider community about the benefits of physical activity?

3.3 Possible Solutions

By focusing on solutions rather than barriers it is possible to look at additional needs as the aim for the whole experience as shown by the following case study.

Case study one

A group of children with behavioural problems were not accessing physical activity opportunities at lunchtimes as their behaviour caused disruption and fighting. They always wanted to play football, but their skill levels did not enable them to participate fully and poor behaviour was used as their first reaction to be being tackled or losing. Their exclusion from these sessions meant that the children were frustrated and could not vent any 'excess energy' so they interfered with other children's opportunities.

First option: Ban the children from physical activity opportunities at lunchtimes.

Second option: Set up a targeted football club for these children so they can play together, away from others. If they do not behave, it will only be their opportunity that is spoilt.

Although this seems a sensible idea, sadly, in practice, this approach was not proactive enough and therefore did not last long. Leaving the children with no support and no incentive did not help, it just marginalised the group.

Third option: An alternative approach would be to look at the problem from a different perspective. The children clearly had behaviour problems, but a key trigger to their poor behaviour was their skill level and lack of social skills to cope with the situations that arose.

A club was set up, building on the children's enjoyment of football, where they would be provided with football coaching to improve their skill level as long as they took an active part in a social skills opportunity that was set up alongside the football club. The learning was targeted at improving the social and coping skills of the children, using football (and physical activity) as a vehicle. Sometimes this meant actually playing the game or learning skills. Other times it meant discussion groups and role play about situations that arose in football, the playground and in wider society. Fantasy football leagues were created with budgets and points linked to attendance, behaviour and meeting set targets.

All of the approaches outlined above could have worked. It is difficult to predict how children and young people will respond to the challenges they are set and the support they are given. In the above example, the third solution worked very effectively and became a sustainable opportunity within the school. Sometimes the first option will work most effectively but it is the range of solutions that is important. There is no one right answer, just as there is no one 'normal' child!

3.4 A Framework for Differentiation

STEP, STTEP or STTEPP

One simple idea often used within Physical Education, is the STTEPP principle of differentiation. (Originally the acronym started out as STEP – Space, Time, Equipment, People – and was adapted by Pickup and Price [2007] to include an additional T for 'task'. Here, we have added an additional 'P' for 'place'.) This outlines the following six areas which can be altered to make opportunities more or less challenging to the children and young people participating:

Space: the size of an area used

Time: how long is given to perform a task

Task: the learning or activity that needs completing

Equipment: what is being used?

People: who is involved, worked with, or leading the sessions?

Place: where an activity takes place; ie different environment, contexts or settings.

Changes can be made by either increasing or decreasing these factors, or changing what is used. It may be a case of how many or how much, or what is being asked.

 Inclusion: Examples of the STTEPP Framework in Use

Reflective task

Think about the opportunities that you are involved in. How could you change these six areas to make it easier for a child or young person with additional needs?

For example, could you limit the space they played in to make passes shorter? Could you give them more time to create a solution to a problem? Could you give them a different task to the rest of the group? Could you give them a different set of equipment that would make success more likely? Could they work in a smaller group of friends, so that their limited social skills could be developed in a more supportive environment? Where would be the most supportive place for them to be working – in school, in a local club or in a high-pressure competition?

What about those children and young people whose additional needs mean that they need more of a challenge? How could you use STTEPP to support them?

Grouping

As mentioned in *Chapter One*, an aspect of Physical Education and the wider sphere of sport is developing the personal characteristics of children and young people. Working with a mixed group can give many opportunities to sensitively explore issues around ability, equity, character and moral development. Supporting children and young people to work together, regardless of their differences, is a key part of both curriculum provision and that beyond the curriculum.

Groups can be created in a number of ways:

- ability

- common barriers

- form or tutor group, class or 'house' system

- friendship

- gender

- interests

- physical characteristics

- random (numbering, style of trainer, colour of eyes, favourite cereal etc).

Examples

A group of talented participants can be supported within a differentiated environment. Quite often this is by asking them to develop their leadership skills by working with less-able performers. Although this has clear benefits to both parties, the talented youngsters also need to be stretched to achieve their full potential. This can be through community sport provision, but schools have a duty to educate these children and young people in balancing their responsibilities, competition and training schedules (see *Chapter Six* for further discussion).

Children and young people who speak English as an Additional Language (EAL) can benefit from working together in a shared community language. They also need to be able to interact outside of this group and therefore need to work with other peers. Wider groups can, of course, benefit from learning key vocabulary in community languages through their physical education opportunities.

How children and young people are grouped or targeted is important, but this can mask the needs of individuals within those groups. Do all boys like football? Do all girls like dance? Do all talented performers have the same capacity for improvement? Do all children and young people respond in the same way towards competition? Can all five-year-olds sequence the same number of movements? Do all children and young people with visual impairment have the same level of impairment?

How targeted or grouped opportunities are 'marketed' is important and should support the inclusive ethos of the school. 'Football Club for Badly Behaved Boys in Year 7' is not particularly inclusive. How those young people are supported in a 'Football Team Development Club' could well make the difference in terms of future participation. Setting up a 'Netball Practice Session', where the focus is on developing basic skills, is more supportive than just having a 'Netball Club' where the only opportunity is for gameplay.

3.5 Conclusion

This chapter does not set out to suggest that practitioners are not aspiring to do the best for all children and young people. Indeed, on this point, a study by Morley et al (2005) suggests that it is not the aspiration that is a problem, rather the attempts to make the 'ideals' a reality.

Knowing the children and young people with whom you are working is central to an inclusive approach. This goes beyond knowing their name (although this is important), to understanding their abilities, needs and aspirations. Talking to the children and young people themselves, their parents and other people who work with them can create an environment where openness and trust outweigh the difficulties inherent within inclusive practice.

Many of the suggestions for how inclusive practice can be achieved, both within and beyond the curriculum, come down to having the time and focus to teach or coach well. As Griggs (2007) points out, 'many will consider these points as simply being good practice, but therein lays the point'.

The most important factor in ensuring that all children and young people are included in a programme is knowing them and understanding their needs. Furthermore is a need for a clear purpose for all opportunities, so all involved understand the appropriateness of the experiences. Opportunities should be responsive to the needs of all children and young people and to the expertise developed by providers. A consistent approach is always beneficial when working with children and young people, both in terms of opportunities and boundaries, as they can then be seen as fixed markers in their ever-changing world.

Within the chapters in *Section C*, planning plays a central part. This is to ensure that the programme is of a high quality, sustainable and effective. Another benefit of strategically planning the programme beyond the curriculum as thoroughly as the curriculum programme, is that additional needs can be more effectively catered for. *Chapter Four* details why planning is important to the whole programme beyond the curriculum and how the programme can be effectively managed.

Key questions

- What are the most prevalent barriers to participation in your school?

- How do you currently target provision?

- Successfully targeting which target group will make the most difference in your school?

References and further reading

Coates, J. and Vickerman, P. (2008) 'Let the children have their say: a review of children with special educational needs and their experiences of Physical Education', *British Journal of Learning Support*, 23(4): 168–175.

Green, K. (2000) 'Extra-Curricular Physical Education in England and Wales: A Sociological Perspective on a Sporting Bias', *Physical Education and Sport Pedagogy*, 5(2): 179–207.

Griggs, G. (2007a) 'Looking on from the sidelines: Inclusion in Primary Physical Education', *Physical Education Matters*, 2(1): vii.

Morley, D. et al (2005) 'Inclusive Physical Education: teachers' views of including pupils with Special Educational Needs and/or disabilities in Physical Education', *European Physical Education Review*, 11(1): 84–107.

Penney, D. and Harris, J. (1997) 'Extra-curricular Physical Education: More of the Same for the More Able?', *Sport, Education and Society*, 2(1): 41–54.

Pickup, I. and Price, L. (2007) *Teaching Physical Education in the Primary School: A Developmental Approach*. London: Continuum International Publishing Group Ltd. ISBN: 978-0-826487-60-2.

Andrews, C. (2005) *Meeting SEN in the Curriculum: PE/Sports*. London: David Fulton Publishers. ISBN: 978-1-843121-64-0.

Hayes, S. and Stidder, G. (2003) *Equity and Inclusion in Physical Education and Sport*. London: Routledge. ISBN: 978-0-415282-26-0.

Stewart, D. (1990) *The Right to Movement: Motor Development in Every School*. London: The Falmer Press Ltd. ISBN: 978-1-850005-27-8.

Vickerman, P, (2007) *Teaching Physical Education to Children with Special Educational Needs*. London: Routledge. ISBN: 978-0-415389-50-1.

Chapter four

Project Management and Monitoring Impact

4

In this chapter you will find:

- why it is important to research current and possible opportunities

- project management principles

- ideas to help evidence impact in your programme.

4.0 Introduction

It is essential, both for the early development of extended programmes and for their sustainability, that every step is taken to plan and evaluate all aspects of the provision. Each school will use a variety of approaches to design, plan and deliver a programme beyond the curriculum. These will vary due to the ethos of the school, its type, size, development stage of the programme and skills within the learning community.

Within this chapter, three stages are promoted as being essential to an effective programme of learning beyond the curriculum: research; management; and monitoring. All must be carried out within an overall plan as they rely on each other for information in order for the next stage to proceed. Research entails finding out what is already happening and what can possibly happen; management covers the planning and delivery stages; while monitoring must be a continual process at all stages.

Without effective management and monitoring, a successful programme is either the result of luck, perseverance or a very charismatic leader. For a programme to develop into a sustainable, dynamic and comprehensive range of opportunities, there needs to be a clear purpose and plan of how to achieve those aims.

There are many reasons why schools do not employ effective management and monitoring techniques, including a lack of:

- auditing and research skills and techniques – the ability to ask the right questions

- time to complete research and compile results

- understanding and experience of designing appropriate programmes from results

- established practice of disseminating findings to the school community

- experience of designing and adapting suitable monitoring tools for use by the whole learning community

- time to implement monitoring systems, collate information and report on findings.

The following sections outline some of the key principles behind management and monitoring that seek to reduce some of the barriers listed above.

4.1 Research

Research is about the search for truth; about finding out what is going on. It is one of the most important factors in providing an effective programme. Findings may not always show what is wanted or needed, but they should be honest; only through informed reflection can true progress be made. Firstly, it is important to audit current practice to find out what opportunities are already in place and what is working effectively. This can help immensely when expanding programmes as building on success is important and it is unlikely that no provision is currently available. Secondly, finding out what is possible in the parameters of the particular learning community is also essential. It would be wonderful to think that a school may attempt to put all of the ideas in this book into action, but that really would take a lot of time and energy to develop and sustain. Being realistic in a programme is a key factor and researching possibilities thoroughly can help keep things realistic.

 ## Monitoring 1: Audit of Opportunity Types

Researching current practice

Without knowing what is already happening there is the danger of creating confusion, repetition and overlap. Auditing current provision should be one of the first tasks undertaken by a learning community. If this is not done, how can it be certain that development is needed or possible?

As well as finding out what is already happening as part of a programme, an audit gives insight into who has been involved and what records have been kept. If nothing has been monitored, an audit may be simply having a conversation with someone else. An audit should look at all aspects of an existing programme including what is on offer, when it is offered, attendance figures and any budgets. It should also try to find out who attends, who does not attend and why. This will mean exploring many sources by talking to school staff, members of an existing learning community, parents, children and young people.

 ## Monitoring 4A and 4B: Registers (Attendance and Evaluation)

Reflective task

Think about how you could find evidence about what you are currently doing, and what works most effectively in terms of existing opportunities.

- When would be the best times of day for new opportunities?

- When do most children and young people attend?

- What marketing of the programme has been successful and why?

- Which target groups have been identified?

- Which coaches and session leaders have been effective and most suitable?

It may be just as likely that this information is easily accessible or that no one knows. This is why an audit is important. Finding out what is happening can also create a strong case for the next stage of research: finding out what else could be done.

Researching possibilities

Researching the possibilities can be the most enjoyable part because it should not be a limiting exercise. Possibilities will be reduced to probabilities during the project management phase, so this is the time to enjoy looking at what might be practicable. Even if finance or other factors indicate a full idea cannot be realised, part of it may be viable and therefore should be considered as a possibility rather than discarded completely.

The following questions give an idea of the range of areas that you will need to explore:

- What is happening in the Physical Education curriculum that would benefit from being extended or enriched?

- Are activities appropriate to the developmental stage of the children or young people that are being targeted?

- What would the children and young people like?

- What are other local schools doing in their programmes that might work in your setting?

- What expertise is there among parents and teachers within the learning community?

- What is being provided in the local community that the school could be linked with?

- What funding opportunities might be available to support the programme?

- What facilities might be available for the school to use?

Finding out the information from the individuals and groups above also means the whole learning community will need to be involved in terms of finding answers and asking the questions. Canvassing views from a range of parties can avoid later frustration when someone says, 'if only I'd known' or 'why didn't you ask?'.

For some of the information, more formal research may be necessary by accessing specific resources, such as the Internet, books (like this one) and journals. Higher education institutions can be a valuable member of the learning community in this aspect. Designing questionnaires and completing data collection exercises may also be necessary, which is discussed more in a later section.

By asking and answering these questions, a plan will start to form. Once this begins, project-management techniques will need to be employed, so that possibilities can become realities.

 Monitoring 2: SWOT Analysis Templates

4.2 Effective Management

Managing a project is an ongoing, reflective process, but it needs to be developed within and against boundaries. Although boundaries are often imposed by cost, time, venues or expertise, perhaps the most important aspect of the success or failure of a project is the support of the senior leaders within the school. An early plan is important, but before time and effort is spent on it, a meeting is needed with those leaders. Could they agree in principle to the idea? If they intend to do so, they will want to know the impact you hope for and the benefits to the children, young people and wider community. Then there will be a period of negotiation regarding timescales, budgets and other key factors. It is important to be prepared for this negotiation and know how far the project plan can compromise before it becomes unworthy of pursuit.

The flowchart below gives a basic process to consider:

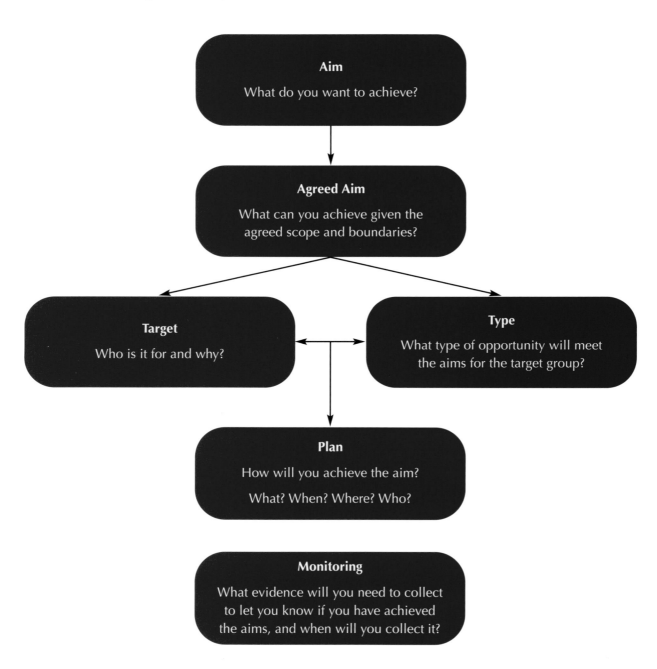

Figure 2: Project management flow chart

The aim and the agreed aims will emerge as a result of the research and negotiation stages. The plan is the way forward in achieving the agreed aim or aims.

Knowing where compromise can be reached and pitching a realistic plan helps negotiations. Make sure the plan is marketed in terms of benefits to the entire school community and how it links to school and wider priorities; having support from colleagues, children and parents can also show that the project may work. It is important to consider how involvement in the project may affect the ongoing business of the school. School leaders will need to know they are supporting a worthwhile and feasible venture.

There are key details that need to be included in a plan to develop either the whole programme of learning beyond the curriculum or single opportunities. Therefore, all aspects of the plan must link to the overall aims and outcomes that are to be achieved.

Here are some suggested areas to consider for the programme proposal and plan:

- links to curriculum learning

- format of event(s)

- timings of event(s)

- space/facilities required

- resources needed, including human resources

- planned timescales

- prior learning from earlier events

- risk assessment

- budget and sources of income

- roles and responsibilities

- contingencies

- communication pathways

- learning community involvement

- monitoring and impact-measurement arrangements.

Within an overall development plan there will be individual strategies for establishing specific opportunities. It may be that over a period of a few years a range of opportunities will be implemented, each building on the opportunities and learning that have preceded it. Effective monitoring will help in ensuring these plans are kept on course and also support the continuation and realisation of those and future plans by providing evidence of impact.

4.3 Evidencing Impact

The success of a programme can be measured in lots of different ways and it is important these measurements illustrate how aims have been achieved and the impact upon the children and young people the programme serves. This is the type of data that can be used in future to engage more support, particularly of the financial kind. Head teachers, school and community leaders will all want to know how the time and effort has been spent and what outcomes for the children, young people, school and community have been met.

It is important to stay focused on the aims of the programme and be pragmatic about what can be monitored. It is also essential to remain realistic about potential impact and modest about the outcomes. Information, particularly numerical data, taken out of context can be interpreted to show positive or negative results. Care must be taken and the method must be agreed at the planning stage of the programme. In addition to helping to evaluate the programme, monitoring can also identify new targets, goals and developments.

Collecting data

Information should be collected to answer a specific question, otherwise it can be meaningless. Questions should be linked to the aims of the programme or opportunity, and consider a variety of types of impact. Information can come in many different forms and from many different members of the learning community. Some examples are:

- registers for sessions

- practitioner self-evaluations

- random, representative or targeted questionnaires for children and parents

- questionnaires or discussions with class teachers and teaching assistants with regard to the impact of the programme on children or young people in class

- attendance and punctuality records of children and young people at school

- reviews of incident books to monitor whether attendance has had a positive impact on the children and young people

- formal assessment of children and young people's progress while attending the programme.

 Monitoring 3: Questionnaires

The data collected may be in the form of numbers, percentages, ideas, words or feelings. It can be quantified or qualified. A balance is suggested as a variety of data will provide a much richer picture of outcomes and impact. Sometimes a numerical difference can be the best indicator of change, while at other times a change in language or attitude can point to a more powerful shift than an isolated figure.

Establishing procedures and systems for data collection will assist in consistency of results and assessment. This information can assist in the future planning of programmes and in monitoring the progress of individual children. It can also substantiate the school's and the learning community's decisions about programmes. Evidence is needed to show value for money in terms of time, expenditure and facilities.

When agreeing an initial plan, those responsible for monitoring and the appropriate methods of doing so should be identified. Individuals responsible for monitoring may include: the school's extended provision coordinator; an Information and Communication Technology (ICT) technician; school administrators; the Physical Education coordinator; and members of senior management. Recognising who is available to lend support is important, as this task cannot be completed by one person.

All groups involved in the programme should also be involved in the monitoring process. This includes the children who attend the opportunities as well as those who choose not to. You should also involve administrators, session leaders and helpers, volunteers, parents and teachers. Remember, the more the whole learning community is involved in the programme, the greater the sense of ownership they will have.

It is important that a range of outcomes is monitored as the learning, development and experiences involved will be specific to the individuals. As discussed in *Chapter One*, Physical Education can provide an array of potential benefits and outcomes for children and young people. These will include physical as well as social, emotional and cognitive benefits. Outcomes that may be measured include:

- changes in activity participation patterns

- changes in positive behaviour

- enjoyment levels of the activities

- gains in confidence and self-esteem from attending the activities

- improved attendance and punctuality of the children and young people at school

- improved communication skills with peers and teachers

- learning from the activities

- making new friends

- transference of skills and knowledge to, and from, the curriculum.

There may also be more concrete measurements, such as the number of children and young people attending clubs, amount of time spent being active, distances walked or even number of competitions won. Although these can clearly be important outcomes in terms of health and sport, it is the broader effects that should really matter to an inclusive Physical Education extended programme.

Analysing data

It is essential to know, when gathering any data, how the data will be utilised to answer the questions being asked. It is possible to collect too much data and time and effort is often wasted in this way. Once a clear question has been articulated and an appropriate method found to collect answers, the next stage is analysis.

Findings should be communicated in the most effective way for the audience it is intended to inform or engage; this may be by means of translation or a variety of formats or methods of presentation. Data may be presented as raw data or interpreted to show percentages or mean averages. It may be converted into tables, charts, graphs, pie charts or any number of data presentation techniques. Whichever method is chosen, achievement of the following points is essential: accurate interpretation and clarity of communication.

As previously mentioned, data can be interpreted to suggest almost anything. For data to be useful it needs to be collected and analysed objectively and without prejudice to the outcomes. If data is misused, it becomes worthless and will not be trusted. If data is analysed robustly and objectively then the power of its message should not be lost in communication.

The additional time taken may seem excessive, but this can make the difference between an extended programme that is engaged with traditional provision or one that just adds to its inequalities.

Making changes

There is no point in collecting and analysing data if it is not going to be used to improve the programme. The principle advocated within this book is that provision, both within and beyond the curriculum, should be built around the needs of the children and young people it involves. Children and young people change and develop over time, so programmes need to adjust to the changes in their abilities, needs and interests. Provision should be altered to ensure freshness of the programme. Data can show what should be changed and provide alternatives.

Change is not as simple as swapping football for cricket or street dance for salsa. The type of activity is not necessarily the most important factor. The whole range of who, what, where, when, how and why questions need to be asked. When changes are suggested, agreed and implemented using the same process as original plans, further monitoring still needs to be incorporated. Ongoing reflection is part of the process to ensure a developmentally appropriate programme. For example, a school may audit staff skills, interests and expertise, and if those do not match the activities on offer then outside providers may be engaged. Over time, staff may develop further experience, which can be harnessed. Similarly, staff may have interests in non-traditional activities, such as martial arts, yoga or korfball. These activities could be incorporated into a programme that could expand possibilities, reduce costs and enhance the learning community. Utilising teachers can also add value to the programme by drawing on their relationship with and the increased understanding of the children and young people.

Change can be difficult to manage if all the learning community have not been fully engaged and involved in agreeing the school vision. If there is disagreement about why opportunities are being established, data can serve as a strong evidence base for decisions. This needs to be carefully managed and a shared understanding of the issues should be encouraged at an early stage.

Case study two

This example shows how one school formulated their programme through researching and evaluating their present programme.

The school's vision was to engage all children with the school's extended learning programmes. Initially, the head teacher recruited a specific member of staff to review the current programme through observations of the activities, assessing their relevance with the present curriculum and links with local community activities. The children and young people's behaviour and competence were other factors recorded through observation.

Questionnaires were distributed to the children and their parents to gain their views on current and new activities for future programmes. Every parent or guardian was also sent a letter stating the school mission in respect to future provision of Physical Education beyond the curriculum in the school. This was to engage parents with the process, canvass their ideas and allow them to contribute to the planning process.

The next stage was to identify the strengths of the school staff, teachers, teaching assistants, nursery nurses, administration, school keeper and lunchtime supervisors to discover which activities could be covered internally. In addition, potential members of the learning community were located and assessed in terms of their suitability to contribute to the school's programme. External facilities were also investigated and prices negotiated to allow the programme to go beyond the school's boundaries and establish school-to-community links.

On reviewing all the data collected, the school devised an appropriate programme for all children within the school. The school stated that each child should attend a minimum of one, and maximum of three sessions per week. In the response letter, parents indicated their support for the programme, agreeing that the programme was in addition to the curriculum and would require some financial input from parents. Obviously, some activities were more expensive than others, though the school offered bursary support for families with financial difficulties and reduced rates to families with more than one child in the school. Parents were informed of the timetable of activities by letter and via the school website several weeks prior to the start of the new programme. Each activity allowed a limited number of participants to ensure high-quality learning, so registration systems had to be established weeks beforehand. On enrolment, parents and guardians received receipt of payment with a voucher for the activity they had requested, detailing the day, time and venue for attendance.

Monitoring of the sessions was integral to delivery to ensure the quality of provision. Each term the information gathered would assist in the redesign of the programme.

Table 2: Example activity programme in a primary school

	Before School	Lunchtime	After School
Monday	Y1/2: Circus skills Y3–6: Invasion	Y1/2: Send and receive Y3/4: Ball games Y5/6: Climbing	Y1: Dance Y3/4: Multi-skill Y5/6: Fencing, football or leadership academy
Tuesday	Y1/2: Fundamentals Y3/4: Dance Y5/6: S&F games	Y1–4: Travelling Y5/6: Ball games	Y1: Playzone Y2–4: Dance Y5/6: Netball and table tennis
Wednesday	Y1: S&F Y2, 5/6: N&W games Y3/4: Coordination	Y1/2: Climbing Y3/4: N&W Y5/6: Multi-skill	Y1: Dance Y2: Invasion Y3/4: Playzone Y5/6: Gymnastics, swimming or tag rugby
Thursday	Y1: S&F Y2: N&W Y3/4: Invasion Y5/6: Dance	Y1/2: Multi-skill Y3/4: Climbing Y5/6: Dance	Y1: Game play Y2: Dance Y3/4: Invasion Y5/6: Multi-skill academy
Friday	Y1: S&F Y2: N&W Y3/4: Invasion Y5/6: Multi-skill	Y1/2: Dance Y3/4: Multi-skill Y5: Invasion Y6: Outdoor adventure	Y5/6: Basketball and urban activities

Key:

- Invasion games (eg football, netball, hockey, basketball, rugby)
- S&F: Striking and fielding games (eg cricket, rounders, softball and baseball)
- N&W: Net and wall games (eg volleyball, tennis, table tennis, badminton).

4.4 Conclusion

When establishing a programme beyond the curriculum, there are three main steps to follow. Begin by auditing provision and researching possibilities, then agree the aims and allow the project to be managed by all of the learning community. Throughout this process, careful monitoring should be carried out so that evidence of impact can be used to improve the future programme. Clear communication is essential throughout the process so the programme can be managed effectively, and the impact can not only be measured, but felt by the children and young people involved.

In summary:

- Find out what your school already does and what it could possibly do

- Decide and agree what you want and what is possible to achieve

- Decide and agree how this can be achieved

- Consider how best to monitor progress

- Do it

- Enjoy it

- Move it forward.

The chapters in *Section C* provide ideas to consider in four particular areas: out-of-school-hours learning; competitive activities; everyday opportunities; and special opportunities. The chapters examine possible barriers to establishing these types of opportunities and suggest potential solutions to overcome these common barriers.

Key questions

- Do you know exactly what provisions your school is currently providing?

- Do you know what opportunities are available in your local community?

- How do you plan your extended programme?

- What evidence do you have about your current programme?

 References and further reading

Bell, J. (2005) *Doing Your Research Project*. Buckingham: Open University Press. ISBN: 978- 0-335215-04-1.

Cohen, L. et al. (2007) *Research Methods in Education*. London: Routledge. ISBN: 978-0-415368-78-0.

Creswell, J. (2008) *Research Design Qualitative, Quantitative and Mixed Methods Approaches*. London: Sage. ISBN: 978-1-412965-57-6.

Chapter five
Out-of-School-Hours Learning

In this chapter you will find:

- different types and the purpose of out-of-hours learning

- common barriers to extended programmes

- ideas about how barriers can be overcome.

5.0 Introduction

The hours just before and just after school curriculum time can be ideal for expanding extended programmes, as children and young people are on the school site, often arriving early or leaving late. This is also an area where many schools have already developed their opportunities. There is much emphasis placed on how much time children and young people spend engaged in physical activity, either for health or other outcomes. Although this is an important factor when considering long-term physical activity habits and skills, it is arguably more important that children and young people receive a broad and varied range of activities rather than just lots of activity (Green, 2004). This is also reflected in the varied nature of physical activity participation throughout a person's lifespan (Penney and Jess, 2004).

A variety of activities should be offered, each type providing a different challenge to the knowledge, skills and understanding of the children and young people. It is this range of opportunities and experiences that will prepare them for future participation and overcoming any barriers to their participation. Even if children and young people choose to focus on one type of activity, for the programme to be considered inclusive, it must show a breadth of opportunity.

Some examples of activities for out-of-school-hour opportunities include:

- **athletic activities** (eg field or track athletics, rollerblading, skateboarding, triathlon)

- **aquatic activities** (eg canoeing, diving, sailing, swimming, water polo)

- **dance activities** (eg ballet, ballroom, disco and latin)

- **fitness activities** (eg aerobics, boxercise, circuit training, walking)

- **gymnastic activities** (eg cheerleading, gymnastics, trampolining)

- **individual (or paired) sports** (eg badminton, golf, rowing, squash, table tennis, tennis)

- **martial arts** (eg aikido, capoeira, judo, karate, taekwondo)

- **non-activity specific** (eg ball, core or multi-skills, team building)

- **outdoor challenge** (eg abseiling, climbing, orienteering, trekking)

- **team sports** (eg basketball, cricket, football, handball, hockey, netball, softball, rugby league or union, volleyball).

The selection of activities should be based on answers to the following questions:

- Will the activity:

    - meet the needs of the children and young people

    - engage the targeted children and young people

    - be possible to run and sustain?

- Are there exit routes and pathways for the children and young people?

This overview of out-of-hours learning is integral to children and young people's development as it allows a direct extension of curriculum learning. Some of the main benefits of targeted opportunities include:

- a motivation to attend

- groups of similar abilities or interests

- more time to gain mastery or establish habits

- smaller numbers

- specific aims to focus.

The main, practical limitation of targeting opportunities is that hard-to-reach groups are, by definition, hard to reach. Attracting target groups can prove frustrating, which is why a broad range of opportunities is so important.

Schools are not, and cannot, be the sole providers of education or physical activity within children's upbringing. Families and community play far more significant roles than schools, and it is this view that suggests why a positive extended programme is so vital. In creating a wide variety of opportunities involving the whole learning community, a programme can mirror a child's experience as he or she develops throughout life. Children and young people develop along a common path, but at very different rates and towards different potentials. Their physical, social, emotional and cognitive developments are related, but these aspects are not necessarily dependent on each other. Children and young people require nurture to impact on nature to ensure their full potential is reached.

Extended programmes are of great importance for the most able and the least able child in equal measure. The talented child requires further opportunities to develop his or her skills, possibly in areas that are not as prominent in the curriculum while the less-able children may need assistance to improve their fundamental skills and enable them to cope with the demands of the curriculum and beyond. Furthermore, developing children and young people's social, cognitive, emotional and creative skills are as important as developing physical skills.

As mentioned earlier, most schools already offer after-school opportunities, either in physical activity or wider learning opportunities. The principles within this chapter relate to all types of out-of-hours learning.

Physical Education opportunities should be seen as an integral part of the overall programme. This way, children and young people can expect consistent standards and make links between curriculum learning and that which lies beyond, as well as the different opportunities within an extended programme. Looking at Physical Education as an entirely separate part of a school's provision can weaken its educational value rather than enhance it.

In addition to the need for a wide variety of physical activities within an out-of-hours programme there is also a need for a variety of opportunities. Out-of-hours opportunities are often considered clubs and their overriding purpose can fall into a number of categories. The table below provides some examples:

Table 3: Different types of club and purpose

Club Type	Club Purpose
Enhancement	Directly builds on curriculum learning, adding depth and time for understanding and mastery of curriculum opportunities.
Enrichment	Adds new experiences or opportunities to those experienced within the curriculum, such as specialist techniques and tactics.
Extension	May be considered for the more able and could constitute representative team practices or advanced skill development.
Encouragement	Mainly to provide motivation, enjoyment, fun and participation. Offers fresh challenges or new opportunities.
Enablement	Provides additional time to support curriculum learning. Gives time to boost skills or develop skills needed to access further opportunities.
Multi/Dual	May be run with two or more target groups involved; for example, clubs run with young leaders supporting the lead practitioner in providing practice and learning for others.

5.1 Possible Barriers

Several significant barriers can limit the effectiveness and scope of an out-of-hours programme. These include:

- lack of purpose

- time

- space

- finance

- personnel.

There is no right or wrong **purpose** of an out-of-school-hours opportunity. Problems only arise if the purpose is not matched to need or is not communicated effectively. Problems can also occur if the purpose that is communicated is not sustained. This might mean children or young people start out at a club and become disillusioned because they were promised one type of club but are provided with something different. Children and young people may be encouraged to attend all opportunities only to discover they do not have the required skills or experience, or even the desire to gain the most from the club.

Although this book advocates more **time** for opportunities through an extended school day, there are clearly many barriers to achieving this. Some children and young people cannot stay beyond the school day for a number of reasons, including travel arrangements, responsibilities as carers, or fatigue after a long day. These are all legitimate barriers and it takes sensitivity and a real understanding of those children and young people's needs to overcome them.

Finding **space** to hold additional opportunities can also cause problems. School sites are often not custom built for modern education and space is at a premium. Appropriate surfaces, access and specialist areas are often unavailable to most schools and it is unlikely funding is able to extend these opportunities greatly. Certain activities (eg climbing, swimming, trampolining and sailing) require specific facilities to enable them to function and cannot run without specialised or specific space. Planning multiple opportunities can also stretch space and facilities; if there is only one indoor space and two different target groups need that space, compromise will be necessary.

Finance provides another barrier to extending a programme of opportunities beyond the curriculum. Costs can be incurred for equipment, facilities and personnel as well as many other eventualities. While curriculum provision can be funded directly from school budgets, they are unlikely to stretch to extended provision. These are optional extras. Some schools, particularly when using external providers, require children and young people to pay or at least contribute towards costs and, although there is certainly a case for contributions being made in terms of ensuring commitment, this can lead to serious inequalities within a programme.

Although there may be many **people** within a learning community with the necessary skills, expertise and time to help, they may not be engaged fully or may not want to be involved. For some, the reason might be availability, for others, the need to bring in money. Other problems may be that appropriate personnel cannot be located. Reliability is a key need, which is often difficult to ensure within a voluntary capacity. There will also be many people within the staff of a school who could contribute; however, a teacher's time is often protected within workload agreements. Teachers may offer to run clubs, but then there are considerations about equity. If external providers are paid, why should school staff be expected to give their time freely?

Though the list may extend beyond the points raised above, one further significant barrier that needs to be taken into account is that of the children and young people's families. Whatever the reason, be it culture or community expectations, some children and young people are not encouraged to participate in physical activities beyond the curriculum. Not even the best planned and designed programme will succeed if no one attends.

5.2 Potential Solutions

With regard to extending a programme, the problems identified above can be seen either as barriers or brick walls. If a learning community truly believes in the aims they have agreed then solutions must be investigated and problems seen as part of the process rather than the end. Not all of the following solutions will fit any one school; they should all be seen as part of a creative response to barriers and may open up more locally appropriate possibilities.

Establishing and communicating purpose

Differences of opinion about the purpose of an out-of-hours programme can cause major delays in establishing an extended programme. At the start of any process of change or development, it is essential that the whole learning community is consulted and informed about why developments are needed. Linking back to *Chapter Four*, this is why evidence is so important in the whole process. Ensuring a shared understanding of the purpose at an early stage can help, but sometimes it is also necessary to remove negative influences from the process. If people cannot contribute towards the shared vision then perhaps it would be more appropriate if they did not contribute at all. This is a hard message, but one that is important in the overall development of the programme.

It is recommended that the school has a development plan and policy for the extended programme, of which the policy for out-of-hours learning will be integral. The programme needs to be developmental through the stages of physical, social, cognitive and emotional maturity to ensure opportunities are appropriate to the needs of the children and young people. This may not sound like the most exciting way to grab opportunities, but in terms of sustainability and impact it is necessary.

The programme should aim to include all year groups within the school and opportunities should progress through these years. Making links to curriculum learning, community learning and other opportunities will help children and young people to see the whole picture. It will also ensure that the learning community understands the value of what they are contributing towards.

Perhaps the two most important groups to engage with for the purpose of a programme are the potential participants and their parents or carers. Parents need to understand that the opportunities are being run for a clear purpose, not just as childcare or to amuse the children and young people. The activities need to be valued by the parents if the children and young people are to receive the support they need. Children and young people need to be able to make informed choices about which opportunities they want to attend and their expectations in terms of content, focus and outcomes.

Using time effectively

Time is a precious commodity and a programme needs to be well planned and structured so time can be used most effectively. This works on both the amount of time within an out-of-hours club and the time spent establishing and monitoring such clubs. Expectations and arrangements for changing into appropriate sportswear should be set out within information letters so that time can be maximised. If a member of the learning community can be available to collate equipment or carry out registers before activities start, this can also limit wasted time. Additionally, involving children and young people in organising warm-ups or setting up drills or other activities can maximise time spent. It is also important to be realistic about what can be achieved within a session and what children and young people can cope with either before or after a school day. Accounting for time for them to change out of their sportswear, so that they can be picked up or arrive at lessons promptly, is also vital.

Timetabling of sessions is another point to consider. Questions arise within an inclusive and developmental programme about the appropriateness of running one type of club the whole year round. Although the same group of children or young people may attend a club every week of the school year, this does not necessarily enable others to use the facilities and time or allow those participants to access other opportunities, as they feel loyal to the original club. Some opportunities may be seasonal, in that they tend to be played only in the summer or the winter, whereas others now seem to be played all year round. It is important to remember that a school's programme does not need to be tied to a professional sports calendar and should be planned to meet the needs of children and young people. Specific opportunities can be developed to lead up to important sporting events and response can be made to major events. This is why a long-term plan is needed, so that all factors can be considered in advance.

Finding space

Environments and facilities differ from school to school, so plans must be specific to each school and community. Space needs to be looked at creatively and researching facilities beyond the school boundaries may open up new possibilities. Some activities will need to be adapted to be possible within a specific facility; however, if this results in the activity being changed beyond recognition, perhaps it should not be used.

It is worth considering the possible facilities that can be used when agreeing aims for the programme as this can be a significant limiting factor. If a school has a hall, a playground and a field then, presumably, three clubs could be run each day (weather permitting, of course!). Thought needs to go into how these spaces can be divided. A small playground may not house two large team games focusing on match play, but it may cope with a skills session and a team-building opportunity. The space available will dictate in some ways how many children and young people can attend a club, so it needs serious consideration.

Finance

Financing out-of-hours programmes raises concerns for all schools and clubs. Though there is no single answer, several avenues to raise funds need to be pursued. As mentioned earlier, charging children and young people to attend clubs can ensure commitment from some, but also exclude others. A bursary system could be implemented for certain children or young people for whom attendance would be truly beneficial, but finance creates too high a barrier. If people understand why charges are included in relation to the quality of what is being offered, they might be more prepared to pay. Expectations rise as payment increases so payments should be directed towards making the opportunity sustainable through purchasing equipment, kit or training personnel.

Another approach is to access local charities through the school governing body or national funding sources. It is vital to have a well-prepared proposal, focusing on impact and its intended outcomes. If charities can see that a project is well planned and has a chance of making a difference to children and young people, they may be more likely to support it. Sports governing bodies also release funds to develop links between clubs and schools, while local community groups and businesses may also be able to support in different ways.

The school itself may be able to target funds at particular opportunities by accessing funds through Parent Teacher Associations (PTAs), sponsored events or the school council. The more creative and impact-focused these opportunities are the better.

The right personnel

Much of the information about finding the right personnel is included within *Chapter Two*. It is important to note, however, that the best planned, targeted, resourced or advertised club can be made worthless if the children and young people do not engage with the session leader. Monitoring all aspects of provision is important, but the interaction between session leaders and participants is, arguably, the most important.

Questionnaires, registers and observations will give some ideas as to how this relationship is developing from both perspectives. Looking at planning, results, performances and other learning outcomes can also help in telling you why those children and young people attending the session feel they are getting something from the interaction. It is just as important to find out this information from those who do not participate or from session leaders who do not remain within the learning community. Identifying what could have been done better will help improve provision.

Case study three

The following highlights the process a primary school underwent to provide an out-of-hours programme for every child within the school.

The head teacher was inspired to extend children's learning beyond the curriculum and utilise the whole school day. His first act in implementing this vision was to identify a suitable member of staff to oversee the programme and, after canvassing every member of staff, child and parent to ascertain their ideas, a policy and plan was devised. The selected staff member compiled the research and presented a report to the head teacher, school staff, children and parents.

The next stage was to identify and contact the learning community, within and beyond the school boundaries, to assist in planning and delivering the out-of-hours programme. This process ensured all parties were informed of the school's policy and vision, and, in this way, gained their support.

Another staff member collated the possible activities and proceeded to plan the timetable, utilising the time prior to school, during break times and after school to ensure that all children gained access to the activities offered by the programme. Identifying children who had prior commitments after school was also important, so that they could be targeted for other times during the school day.

The next task was to employ a variety of groups from the learning community and book the use of their facilities. All contributors to the programme signed a service level agreement so that each party recognised its role within the programme. Risk assessments were completed for all activities and session leaders were inducted.

A newsletter was produced to disseminate information to the parties involved, which focused on the extended learning opportunities and incorporated design and content from the children and young people.

Plans to monitor attendance and impact of provision were drawn up and implemented, involving feedback from children and young people, parents and other members of the learning community. The monitoring of the programme highlighted support for the provision and reinforced the reasoning behind delivering such a comprehensive programme. The following comments were included:

- 'I improved my skills so that I was able to succeed in class'

- 'I made new friends with children in the school'

- 'My child has become more confident and willing to try new things at home'

- 'The children are more focused in class and are able to apply themselves longer than before'

- 'The children improved their knowledge and understanding of the activity and are now able to continue playing competitive games for considerable time'.

5.3 Conclusion

When planning to change or develop out-of-hours provision, it is important to know what is being changed or developed. Audit the current programme to see what complements the aims and outcomes of the overall extended programme. Auditing community links at this stage is also essential; you should then develop a sustainable programme by identifying and communicating the purpose, the target groups and the timings ensuring costs and facilities are in place and personnel are fully engaged. Once a programme is ready, be sure to advertise it appropriately to all members of the learning community.

Key questions

• In your school, which children do not currently attend out-of-hours learning and why?

• When is the least popular time of the week for out-of-hours learning?

• Who in your learning community is not yet fully involved in your out-of-hours programme?

 References and further reading

Green, K. (2004) 'Physical Education, lifelong participation and "the couch potato society"', *Physical Education and Sport Pedagogy*, 9(1): 73–85.

Penney, D. and Jess, M. (2004) 'Physical Education and Physically Active Lives: A Lifelong Approach to Curriculum Development', *Sport, Education and Society*, 9(2): 269–288.

Chapter six
Competitive Activities

In this chapter you will find:

- a brief discussion about the educational value of competition

- a summary of the different types, levels and formats of competition

- common barriers to effective competition and some solutions to these barriers.

6.0 Introduction

For many people, competitive activities are, or should be, the main focus of Physical Education within schools. Certainly, many parts of an extended programme may focus on this particular aspect of learning. This book promotes competition within Physical Education provision as being a tool for learning. Children and young people are naturally competitive. They want to see how well they can do and, in time, how well they can do against others. However, competition should not be the sole purpose of an extended Physical Education programme. It should be an experience to learn from and form just part of the whole range of opportunities planned to develop children and young people in this area.

The concept of competition is a contested area. Drewe (1998) writes about there being 'opposing…virtues and vices of competition'. These virtues include the development of character, including dedication, discipline and courage. Competition prepares children and young people for the realities of life and is about the satisfaction of striving together against an opponent. Some of the arguments that counter the importance of competition, focus on the inequalities generated from it and how this can act against educational values. Competition can also be seen to promote a 'win-at-all-costs' attitude, which can lead to cheating and acceptance of immoral acts, such as harming others, abuse of officials or taking illegal substances. Competition is also inherently selfish, in that individuals or teams are acting to do the best for themselves.

The purpose of this chapter is not to counter these arguments. All have some basis in truth, but all need to be considered when establishing a coherent policy and programme for competition in schools. What Drewe (1998) points out is that 'children not only require the physical skills necessary for the competitive activity, but they must also be mentally and socially 'ready''. The learning community needs to be aware of both sides of the argument in order to make relevant adjustments to their practice.

Certainly, the so-called virtues can be developed by participation in competitive activities, just as vices can also manifest within this environment. What is important, from an inclusive perspective, is ensuring that it is not just particular children and young people who achieve the virtues by winning all the time. If it is important for children and young people to learn about competition then they must experience winning and losing in order to fully understand it. This is not to suggest that all children and young people must have a turn at winning as that would negate the competitive experience. What is important is that they are given a chance of winning and this comes from preparedness and competition appropriate to their phase of development. They need a fair chance of winning and losing.

Competition has a variety of effects upon participants. If a child or young person always loses and cannot identify how they could have done any better, this will not be beneficial to their experience. Similarly, if someone always wins without having to try hard, they will become disillusioned. Competition does not inherently incite a positive or negative experience, but how it is used can generate either outcome. Producing competitive opportunities that are fully inclusive and appropriate for the child is a balancing act and preparing children for competitive experiences goes beyond the physical skills and fitness. Children and young people need support in many social, emotional and cognitive aspects of learning related to competition, such as responding to competitive experiences and making the most of the opportunities that are available.

Children and young people should be encouraged to take part in a variety of competitions. This means not only in different activities, but in different types of interaction. There are three main interactions within competition:

- **Direct competition** relates to competition where individuals or teams aim to beat the other participants by being better than them at that particular moment. How this is measured will depend on the particular activity, but may include being the fastest, scoring the most goals or points, or making fewer mistakes. Within direct competition there may also be elements of indirect competition when competitors' results are compared against external markers such as standards, times or distances.

- **Indirect competition** can encompass a variety of competitive challenges. These may include competing against set criteria, particular challenges, times or environmental goals, such as heights or distances. Within indirect competition participants may not compete at the same time, but the challenge or method of judgement will remain constant across performances.

- **Virtual competition** is where two teams or individuals compete indirectly in different venues, but performances are relayed via the Internet or some other electronic means.

Reflective task

What type of competition would you consider a gymnastic event to be? Gymnasts compete one after another to gain the highest score possible from judges against objective criteria. Once all the entrants have competed, the one with the highest score will win.

How about a dance competition, where couples perform in heats and are scored by judges? Again, the contestants with the top scores progress through to the next round.

What type of competition is climbing a mountain? Climbers try to overcome the challenge of the mountain, but also try to do it in a quicker time than previous successful attempts.

Levels of competition

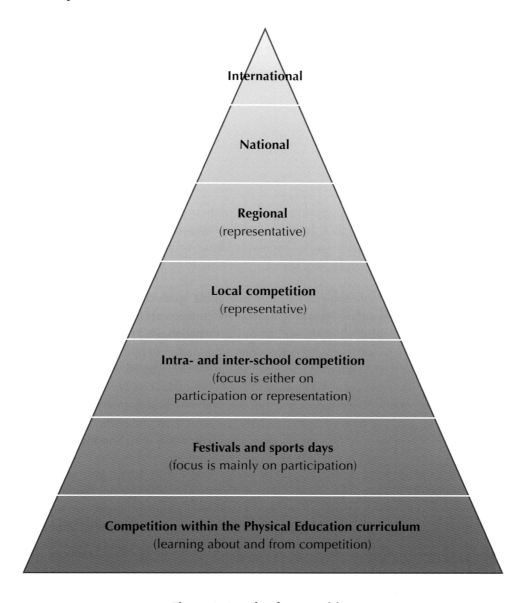

Figure 3: Levels of competition

It is essential that the purpose of a competition is communicated early within the process. Generally, competitions fall into two categories: representative or participatory. The formats of competition described below can fit into either category and can be used to either select the best performers for the next level of competition or to involve all children and young people in competition.

Festivals come under a variety of guises; however, for the purpose of this book, a festival is an event that emphasises the importance of specific skills rather than competition against an opponent. This event leans towards the individual competing against themselves and assessing whether they have improved upon previous scores. The opportunity to engage with other competitors undergoing similar processes will develop the children's skill in working in unfamiliar surroundings, which is important for the children and young people in relation to future challenges.

 Ideas 3: Multi-Skill Festival

Sports day events also have a variety of models, but there needs to be a clearly communicated identity for such a tournament as it seems to be the most significant external event in schools' competition calendars. A 'sports day' should involve a variety of sporting events over the period of one day. These sports should relate to the experiences undertaken through the Physical Education curriculum and result in the opportunity to demonstrate the learning over the curriculum year. This formula is an extension to the festivals, as the skills required are more complex and challenging. It would suit children and young people who have matured in their fundamental movement skills and possess the relevant physical, social, cognitive and personal skills to cope with the events. Activities, particularly sports, should be modified for younger or less-skilful children and young people to ensure they are appropriately challenged.

Different models for a sports day:

- **Athletic festivals** involve running, jumping and throwing events. In primary schools, in addition to a range of running challenges, children and young people should experience a variety of throwing and jumping events that are not discus, javelin, high or triple jump, as the curriculum at that level does not require them. Secondary schools lead young people to perform more traditional track and field events such as discus, javelin, high or triple jump.

  One suggestion that may ensure a greater number of participants would be a rule that each competitor can only enter one running and one field event (jump or throw), plus a relay.

- **A multi-sport approach** would involve a variety of sports that children and young people have experienced during the year, through the curriculum and extended programme. Each young person in the form or class should compete in one event to ensure mass participation and the results across all the sports are collated to give the final score. Each class identifies who is in each team, selecting through discussion in registration periods and beyond, with support from school staff and the learning community. Engaging the children and young people in deciding which event they participate in assists in wider learning.

 Ideas 4: Alternative Sports Day

- **A carousel of events** involves several physical challenge stations that all children complete, relating to the skills learnt previously in Physical Education and extended programme. Demonstrating competence to peers, teachers and parents or carers is important to a child's personal skill development. Each child records his or her performances and gain points for the 'house' team, which are collated at the end to identify the winning team.

- An **individual sport or physical challenge** may involve an outdoor and adventurous event, involving orienteering and problem-solving activities, in small groups against the clock. Another consideration is a specific event that all children and young people compete in, to ensure maximum participation in the activity. For example, a tag rugby event that involves every child in small-sided games, gaining points for the 'house' team from the results of individual matches.

The defining factor of these examples is that they are inclusive and linked with prior learning, so children and young people can demonstrate learning as they do for other subjects by means of exams. These events can be considered as an equivalent to subject exams and if the school policy and development plans highlight this fact, the whole school can contribute to the day.

Intra-school competitions ensure all children access competitions within the boundaries of their school and enable the children and young people to compete in a safe environment among their peers. Such competition can be considered as a prerequisite to competing against other schools, although the experience should not be underestimated and requires careful planning to ensure children and young people are developed through it. The activities should depend on support from the learning community to encourage the children and young people in physical activity opportunities beyond school boundaries. It is recommended that the intra-school competition framework has progression as its central theme, with challenges appropriate to the children's abilities and experience rather than just their age.

Inter-school competitions involve a school competing against another or several schools. Essentially, prior experiences of competition will have taken place, so the children and young people have developed to reach this point. Representing school, club or community is necessary to broaden children's experiences of competition and establishing a clear pathway of development will enable children and young people to engage and thrive on new and challenging experiences. Organisation of these events often comes from the learning community to ensure that the pathway from school to clubs and community is firmly established. The school's responsibility is to establish and prepare the competing individuals or teams and ensure they gain the experience of challenging peers from other schools.

How each of these types or levels of school competition are organised is another way that variety can be added to a competitive programme. There are a number of different formats that are summarised here.

- In **continuous** competitions, fixtures continue at the same level over a period of time. The most obvious example is that of a league where all entrants compete against each other before the overall winner is decided. Leagues may have a home and away basis, where each entrant plays each other twice. It may also be just one fixture between each team (a 'round robin'). Points are awarded for wins and draws and each entrant plays the same number of fixtures.

  The winner is usually at the top of the league at the end of all fixtures, but some leagues end with a 'play-off' where the top few teams play each other at the end of all fixtures to culminate in a final.

- **Progressive** competitions consist of heats or rounds where entrants are knocked out at each stage. These culminate in a final fixture where the winner of that fixture wins the competition overall.

  Entrants are either placed in a draw and the fixtures randomly selected or they are seeded so that stronger entrants cannot play each other until later in the competition.

  Progressive or 'cup' competitions can be extended by having the entrants who were knocked out in the early rounds entering into a 'shield' knockout system. Those eliminated from this level of competition can be entered into a knockout 'plate' system, which increases the number of fixtures played by each entrant and will potentially leave three winners (cup, shield and plate) at different levels.

 Competition 1: Progressive Knockout Competition

- There are several alternatives to direct knockout competition between two entrants at each level; **heats** can be of several entrants who compete to gain the highest score or fastest time. Children with the top scores or fastest times progress to the next round, regardless of from which heat they came.

 Competition 4: Heats

- **Combination** events tend to be organised as continuous competitions that extend further, with the winners moving into a progressive competition. Entrants may be split into two or more 'pools' or leagues, where all entrants within the pools play each other. Like the play-offs of continuous competitions, the top teams from these pools progress into a knockout stage, moving towards a final.

- The **ladder** is a recognised form of organising fixtures; it is not the same as a league as each player does not necessarily play each player or team. In this format, entrants are placed vertically on rungs of a ladder. Entrants can challenge others who are one or two rungs above them. If the lower entrant wins, they change places on the ladder. At the end of a period of time, the top entrant wins the ladder. This may result in promotion to a higher ladder. If only one ladder is being used, after a certain period the ladder can be inverted to set new challenges.

 Competition 3: Ladder

- A **single fixture** is a one-off competition between two entrants where the result stands in isolation from any other result.

- A **series** is several fixtures (usually an odd number) between two entrants over a period of time. Each result of a fixture counts towards the series result; for example, in a 'best-of-five' scenario.

If individuals, pairs or teams of children or young people are competing in competitions, consideration needs to be made as to how these teams are selected. The selection process can be very contentious, particularly if a random or draft method is chosen. A **random** method is simply that names are drawn and put into teams. Although this is fair, based on luck and chance, it does not necessarily create an appropriate level of competition for all children and young people.

Using a **draft** method is perhaps the least valuable method of selecting teams, where captains or managers take turns in choosing who is wanted first. Although this gives some equity in who plays for which team, consider the impact of those who are not picked early or are picked last. They are, explicitly, the least wanted. This may also not reflect a child's ability, potential or wider contribution as it may just come down to his or her popularity or, at worst, lack of it.

Selection will exclude some, but may be necessary, if teams have limited numbers. Having clear reasons for selection or non-selection can help to explain exclusion so that all children and young people enter the process with a clear understanding; criteria and trials are two ways to achieve this. Selection **criteria** may outline prerequisites needed to participate or the level that needs to have been achieved for this type of competition to be appropriate for the children and young people. **Trials** give all interested participants a chance to demonstrate their abilities and aptitudes and those who achieve well are invited to the next stage. It is important with both methods that criteria are established and trials run objectively. Favouritism should not feature as part of the process.

Nominations and commitment or attendance are also alternatives. **Nominations** for selection may come from within the group. Clear criteria should be used and an adult's discretion may be necessary. This may be more useful for choosing captains or specific roles rather than the representatives themselves. For certain competitions it may also be appropriate to reward those who have shown good commitment or attended regularly.

Competitions can be open for anyone eligible to enter or limited to a particular level or **category** such as beginners, intermediate or advanced. This gives all involved an understanding of what the expectations are for the level of competition. Beginners' levels may be specified for those who have been learning a skill for a certain amount of time, whereas advanced level might mean that they have competed at a particular level before. This is another way to ensure appropriate competition.

A final, general point on competitive activities focuses on the competitive activity itself. It is important that these are created, selected or modified to meet the needs of the children and young people. Full-sided, adult versions of sports are not necessarily appropriate to children and young people, so it is quite acceptable, and even encouraged, to modify them as much as is necessary to make the opportunity accessible. This may be by changing equipment, altering rules, numbers of players or any number of features. Many sports' governing bodies (eg The Football Association) have their own formats of sports for particular age groups, although these should be matched to ability levels as well. The children and young people are the most important consideration, not the sport.

 Competition 5: Staff, Volunteer and Spectator Code of Conduct

6.1 Possible Barriers

Many of the barriers to developing provision for competitive activities are similar to those highlighted in *Chapter Five*. In many ways, the organisation of competitive activities and out-of-hours learning are similar, with issues arising in the following four areas: ethos; personnel; knowledge; and cost.

As discussed in the introduction to this chapter, there are many differing opinions as to the educational and wider benefits of competition. Different groups and individuals within the learning community (eg governors, parents, children and young people) may not share the school's view of competition or may disagree with the inclusive philosophy espoused within this book. Competition is an area that is relevant both locally and nationally; the media and government both have strong views about the importance of competition, although neither opinion may be in line with, nor as well considered as, an individual school's policy.

Identifying these groups and their influences upon the school ethos will enable you to identify suitable competitive events with limited barriers. As with national sporting events, it is not necessarily the behaviour of the participants that comes under scrutiny; parents and carers can sometimes take their support to inappropriate levels. Codes of conduct for participants and spectators can be beneficial.

The issues identified within *Chapter Two* are also relevant to competitive activities, although the range of expertise required may be slightly different. A team is needed to support the planning and delivery of the event which may include:

- announcer

- area coordinators

- chaperones

- first aid (clearly marked area for treatment)

- judges/umpires (for each activity for the event)

- marshals (to oversee specific areas, ensure participants are safe from spectators, environment etc)

- photographer

- refreshment sellers

- reporters

- score keepers

- score runners

- time keepers

- volunteers

- welcome/registration party.

It is also important to note that it is the learning community that enforces and establishes the ethos of an event, so they need to be supportive of the agreed aims set out within the overall plan.

Keen and willing volunteers may need support when considering the best type of competitive event to stage. The details in this chapter should help, but agreed rules for events and expectations of those involved should also be considered further.

For larger competitive events, additional financial concerns may be prevalent. Specifically, these may include:

- administration (eg marketing, reprographics, letters)

- certificates (for participants, volunteers, medals, trophies)

- equipment (eg tools for the activities, public address system, uniform, stationery)

- merchandise (eg t-shirts, hats, programmes, bags, badges)

- personnel (eg judges, score keepers, crowd control, information desk, first aid, travel costs for volunteers)

- refreshments (eg for participants, volunteers, employees, spectators)

- venue hire (eg transport, field, sport centre, rooms).

6.2 Potential Solutions

By now, patterns should be evident in how barriers can be overcome. Agreeing appropriate aims, engaging the learning community, planning and monitoring effectively and being creative would seem to be the main solutions repeated throughout this book. In terms of overcoming barriers to competition these remain true, although views on competition are perhaps more strongly held and contested than others mentioned so far.

Providing a broad programme of competitive events can help to achieve the aims of the programme while also engaging different groups. Within an inclusive philosophy, it is possible to have all children and young people accessing different levels of competition as it would not be acceptable to make each child compete at the same level. The levels of competition should meet the needs and abilities of the children and young people taking part.

Adopting a developmental competition framework allows all children and young people to be involved at the start of the competition. This increases their experience and skills and gives them an opportunity to reach their potential, while also identifying those who may benefit from more challenging levels of competition. Beyond physical performance there will be children and young people with other talents who can further their involvement by honing their skills as coaches, reporters, photographers or umpires.

Reflective task

Use the table below to think about your current and potential learning communities. Who might volunteer or could be asked to fulfil the following roles?

	Teachers	Wider School Staff	Children and Young People	Parents	Other Schools and Wider Educational Community	Wider Sporting Community	Wider Community (including businesses)
Administration							
Announcements							
First aid							
Fund-raising							
General aid							
Marshalls							
Media							
Officials							
Pastoral care							
Photography							
Refreshments							
Registration							
Score keepers							

As with any other event, a risk assessment must be completed and particular focus should be afforded to the effects of competition on children and young people. While behaviour may not be an issue in some events, competition is about striving to be the best and all the positive, negative, social and emotional outcomes of competition need to be considered. When planning progressive competitions, issues of the space and layout are also important so heats can be completed without the distraction of others' performances. Consideration should also be shown to how spectators will be able to position themselves and move around the competition area, so designating a specific space for them is often a good idea. Furthermore, it is paramount to establish contingency procedures for an alternative venue or date if poor weather or another outside cause means the event has to be postponed.

 Ideas 2: Fitness Challenge

Any additional physical and emotional stress brought on by the length of time children and young people are expected to compete needs to be factored into plans. This may also relate to the time of the year, week or term, as there are many different experiences and pressures facing children and young people that need to be balanced against their physical activity participation and competition schedule. Exam periods, end of term or school productions are three examples of time when energy may need to be directed elsewhere. Early planning and good communication can alleviate potential problems in this area.

Below are some questions that should be considered at the start of the competition planning process:

- What benefits will competition bring for the children and young people?

- How will it link to curriculum learning?

- How will children and young people be prepared for the event?

- What type and format of competition is most appropriate to the participants' needs?

- What activity/activities will engage the children?

- Is the competition targeted? If not, what different levels or adaptations of competition are necessary to include all children and young people?

- Who, from the learning community, will be able to support the event?

- How will the event be monitored?

Once you have answers to these questions, you can make decisions on the details of when, where, how and what.

Conversely, if an invitation has been received to attend an external competition, the following questions should be considered:

- How does the event link to school plans?

- What type and format of competition is it?

- Which target group of children and young people is being invited?

- Is the competition appropriate?

- What is the timescale for preparation?

- How can the target group be prepared?

- How will success be monitored?

Case study four

It is time for the final festival of the school year, which incorporates the learning community and a number of primary schools within a close geographical area.

Purpose: This is an opportunity for children from each primary school to participate in a 'fitness festival' and test their skills and fitness against other children competing as class groups. The festival will also provide children with access to information about different opportunities within the learning community. In addition, the event will act as a showcase for the benefits of working in partnership with a wide range of providers.

Venue: With all the primary schools to attend, a venue that holds over 700 children is required. The most appropriate venue is a local park with changing and toilet facilities, and secure fencing around the designated area. Each person who assists in the event is provided with a map of the area, with every activity, first-aid and information desk highlighted.

Learning community: Invitations are sent to the local sport clubs, coaching agencies, sports development staff and community groups that operate in the schools and meet quality-assurance standards. Further invites were sent to representatives from Healthy Schools, the primary care trust, local leisure services, secondary schools and the marketing department of the local authority as each can provide expertise within their field to assist with the day.

Table 4: The learning community's involvement in competition

Community Learning Groups	Area of Expertise
Healthy Schools	To provide refreshment (eg fruit smoothies) for every participant
Primary care trust	To provide areas for children to learn about oral hygiene and effects of exercise upon the body through school nurses
Leisure services	To assist in accessing local park and provide staff as volunteers on the day
Local secondary schools	To provide young people to assist on the day for a variety of security roles around the park and assist movement of schools around the carousel
Local authority marketing department	To provide support on reporting the event, including pictures in local papers, prior to and following the event
Local clubs/community groups and sports centre staff	To provide capoeira, football, rugby, netball, tennis, yoga, basketball, athletics and fitness challenge stations
Sponsors	Local convenience store to provide water for every child Local authority to provide funds to assist with event, in addition to staff time.

Case study four (continued)

Key features of the planning process:

- Ensure a shared vision for the event with clear understanding and reasons for providing the opportunity

- Identify and meet all groups within the learning community and recruit assistance

- Establish roles, responsibilities and timelines

- Write to potential sponsors with information on the event, outlining aims, impact and outcomes

- Inform and establish registration system for all primary schools with layout of the day and timings

- Contact local first-aid providers for medical assistance

- Design booklet for the day, with information about the learning community and sponsors, timetable of events and layout of the park for all attendees

- Ensure risk assessment is completed and verified by local authority

- Inform venue security/police of the event and ensure that refuse disposals are readily available to keep park clean

- Meet school volunteers, prior to event, to discuss roles and responsibilities

- Establish questionnaires for schools, children and learning community

- Establish date for self-review with representatives from schools and community learning groups

- Establish date and discuss improvements for the following year's event.

6.3 Conclusion

Competition is a way of adding challenge to an extended Physical Education programme and should be accessible to all children and young people at an appropriate level. It should also be used to ensure children and young people understand how to respond to competitive situations and strive to do their best. Competition, within an inclusive and educative extended Physical Education programme, should not just be about who is the best.

Planning a broad range of competitive activities can help to offer appropriate experiences, extending to and supporting all children and young people in equal measure. Appropriate competition means that the type, format, level and rules are matched to the learning needs and physical, social, cognitive and emotional abilities of the children and young people involved. The term 'appropriate' within direct competition also applies to the opposition. This is one of the reasons staff are not encouraged to compete against pupils (Whitlam and Beaumont, 2008) as this would not be appropriate competition. The benefits of competition need to be balanced with the inherent physical and emotional risks.

Competition is one way of demonstrating the learning that has been achieved within the curriculum, so it should be celebrated by the whole learning community. Where teams or individuals compete on behalf of a school, the results should be communicated to the whole learning community. More ideas linked to this appear in the next chapter, *Everyday Opportunities*.

Key questions

- How do children or young people who compete at a high level also benefit from representing their school?

- What types of competition do you currently have in your school?

- How do you support your children and young people in learning from competition?

References and further reading

Drewe, S. B. (1998) 'Competing Conceptions of Competition: Implications for Physical Education', *European Physical Education Review*, 4(1): 5–20.

Whitlam, P. and Beaumont, G. (2008) *Safe Practice in Physical Education and School Sport*. Leeds: Coachwise Business Solutions. ISBN: 978-1-905540-54-9.

Chapter seven
Everyday Opportunities

7

In this chapter you will find:

- reasons why Physical Education does not happen all day, every day

- ideas on how to integrate Physical Education into everyday school life, including walking, sports councils, cross-curricular links and displays.

7.0 Introduction

Organised clubs, competitions and special events can all raise the status of Physical Education. They also increase the opportunities for children and young people to develop their skills, be physically active and enjoy activity. Earlier chapters within this book have touched upon how to make these opportunities sustainable and embed them in the school's ethos.

This chapter looks at developing opportunities for children and young people to be active and learn about or through activity. Such opportunities lie within current provision beyond Physical Education. If a broader understanding of Physical Education is supported, a wider range of skills and attributes can be seen as having resonance with wider school priorities, such as policies, development plans and both the official and experienced curriculum. Physical Education sets out to develop children and young people as problem solvers and communicators, strategists and leaders, with responsibility and independence. A broader view of learning would clearly complement the learning developed through other curricular subjects well within the aims and overall ethos of a school. Physical activity is the medium through which children and young people can become engaged and motivated.

Developing ideas within this chapter is not about Physical Education being given a higher percentage of time in school, it is about acknowledging the benefits to children and young people that Physical Education can provide.

7.1 Possible Barriers

With a creative eye, there are many opportunities throughout the school day to develop skills and attributes that are considered part of Physical Education. It would be easy to say that the only possible barrier would be a lack of imagination! In reality, however, there are several factors that may limit these opportunities. The most significant of these is **time**. 'I'm so busy, I can't possibly' and 'The day is already so busy, I couldn't...' are familiar excuses. The pressure on schools, and teachers, to 'educate' children tends to focus on the core areas of reading, writing, mathematics, ICT and science. Although the rhetoric of Government and society charges schools with developing rounded and healthy individuals, until society changes the way schools are judged and children tested, 'core' subjects will remain the highest priority for schools.

This links to the **status** of Physical Education within schools. If sport is used as the major justification for the subject, schools could argue against its value to society and education. If exercise and being active are seen as the sole reasoning behind the subject, this further weakens the argument for making it a priority status within education.

It is only when the benefits of Physical Education to the all-round education and well-being of children and young people are seen, that the argument becomes stronger. Physical Education needs to regarded as educational in order to have any sort of status within education.

Everyday opportunities can contribute to a whole host of educational, health and sporting benefits, but only if they are delivered well alongside many other important opportunities for personal, social and intellectual development. If a more humble message can be communicated, with the passion and commitment of those who believe in the importance of all that Physical Education can support, the extra 10 minutes here and there can be found and used well. People need to see and understand the point of what they are being asked to do, as well as what they can do to achieve it.

7.2 Potential Solutions

Walking

After crawling or 'bum-shuffling', walking is one of the first ways children get to independently explore the world outside their immediate grasp. It is also an excellent way to accumulate physical activity at levels beneficial to health. Establishing a walking programme within school or just encouraging more walking on the school site, can be a cheap and sustainable way to increase physical education each day.

A walking route can be measured around the perimeter of the school site or just around a section of the playground or field. This route can be permanently marked, meaning that points of interest or challenges can be set up around the route. These might relate to physical challenges (eg count the number steps for the next 100 metres) or could be linked to a theme, topic or subject.

In limited space a 'star path' may be useful, where each 'arm' of the star is a certain length.

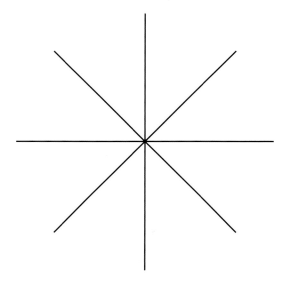

Figure 4: Example of a star path

The children and young people start from the middle and walk to touch each point of the star, returning to the middle after each point. If each arm of the star is 20 metres, the following route will cover 320 metres (which is higher than the Eiffel Tower) and could be a 20-minute walk for a toddler. Clues or information could be collected at the end of each arm.

For longer routes away from the school site, careful consideration would be required regarding risk assessment and also maintaining the children and young people's interest levels. When a route is planned, think about how frequently sites of interest, clues or prizes might be needed. This will link to the overall time and, more importantly, to the motivational levels and attention span of the children or young people.

For a planned walk, it is important to know approximately how far you might expect to travel in a certain time. The table below gives some indication of walking speeds on flat ground.

Table 5: Approximate walking speeds and distances (in metres)

	Speed km/h	10 minutes	15 minutes	20 minutes	30 minutes	40 minutes
Toddler	1	167	250	334	500	750
Child	2	334	501	668	1002	1503
Young person (average)	3	500	750	1000	1500	2250
Brisk	4	667	1000	1334	2000	3000

Challenges can be set on an individual, group, class or school level, encouraging walking over a set distance. If a route is marked out, a certain number of circuits can be equated to any number of routes in the local area or further afield. These may be completed in one session or may take a cumulative effort.

Some interesting approximate distances and heights are included below in Table 6.

Table 6: Distances for walking programmes

Route	Distance (kilometres)	Distance (miles)
A mile	1.61	1
Amazon River	6,400	4,000
Ben Nevis (Scotland)	1.344	0.84
Darwin to Melbourne	3,140	1,962.5
Dover to Calais	34	21.25
Earth to the Moon	360,000	225,000
Eiffel Tower	0.244	0.15
Mt Everest	8.844	5.53
The Equator	40,074	2,504.25
Great Wall of China	8,852	5,532.5
Hadrian's Wall	132	82.5
K2	8.611	5.38
Land's End to John O'Groats (direct)	970	606.25
London to Paris	341	213.13
The M25	188	117.5
A marathon	42.2	26.2
River Thames	344	215
Route 66 (across USA)	3,664	2,290
Scafell Pike (England)	0.978	0.61
Slieve Donard (Northern Ireland)	0.849	0.53
Mt Snowdon (Wales)	1.085	0.68

Walking can be around a simple route or it can involve complex map reading or orienteering skills. It may be for health or enjoyment, to relax, find information or achieve a target. It can be supported by a pedometer or other forms of measurement. Taking a class for a walk can offer wonderful opportunities to talk and reflect; it can also make children more alert and contribute to their health. Not bad for something that does not need to cost anything, except a bit of time to set up.

Assemblies

There are many stories from sport and physical activity that demonstrate people's potential for greatness. There are also tales that show the errors and consequences of decisions that people make. Whole-school or smaller-scale assemblies can be good opportunities to share the inspiration some of these stories can bring.

With sport and physical activity being a fundamental part of many cultures and societies, it can offer opportunities to discuss controversial issues linked to personal, moral and social education. Stories about overcoming or struggling against adversity and challenges can inspire children and young people in all aspects of their lives as well as motivate them to stay involved in physical activity.

Issues such as ethics, cheating and drug-taking are, sadly, all too prevalent within sport, but these offer opportunities to discuss the real-life consequences of such actions and, with older young people, the chance to consider both sides of the debate.

Individuals and debates that, for very different reasons, could be used as examples include:

- Muhammad Ali

- Lance Armstrong

- Arthur Ashe

- Nadia Comaneci

- Dame Tanni Grey-Thompson

- Dame Kelly Holmes

- issues arising from apartheid within South African sport

- Ben Johnson

- Michael Jordan

- Gene Kelly

- Billie Jean King

- Olga Korbut

- Dame Ellen McArthur

- Bobby Moore

- Jesse Owens

- Sir Steve Redgrave

- Michael Watson

- Tiger Woods.

There will also be many individuals and stories from within your local community, or different cultures that may engage children and young people and inspire them to similar actions. How can you use these contacts to make assemblies come to life? Can you arrange visitors to come in and talk to the children or young people? If you choose to do this, it is worth having an agreed 'script' as a foundation to make sure there is no misunderstanding about the purpose and boundaries of the talk and to help structure follow-up work and extending the opportunity (see *Chapter Eight* for more details).

Travel to and from school

Although children, young people and their parents may have limited choices in how they get to school, educating and enabling them to consider active choices should be part of the whole school plan for physical activity.

Is there storage for bicycles? How can a local authority be influenced to consider parking restrictions close to schools, developing cycle paths or 'walking buses'? The latter idea stems from parents and support workers working as a community to 'pick up' children as the 'bus' works its way towards the school. Exploring these possibilities and sharing experiences can open up opportunities. 'Carpooling' is becoming much more common for colleagues travelling to work – is it worth considering for travel to school too?

Most local authorities have staff dedicated to supporting school travel – what ideas do they have? Do they offer incentives, schemes or strategies to support you in this work? With older young people, it may even be possible to organise 'jogging-to-school' groups, although practical implications would need to be considered in terms of safe routes and showering facilities.

Developing responsibility through leadership opportunities

One important group involved in the learning community identified in *Chapter Two* is the children and young people themselves, and giving a sense of autonomy and ownership of opportunities should increase their interest. Developing responsibility is a key part of the education process, so that children who join school can leave as responsible and independent young people. Without independence it will be very difficult to access adult physical-activity opportunities.

The ability to work with others, manage oneself and lead others are essential skills for both Physical Education and life. Helping children and young people to develop these skills is important and, in doing so, can also help develop the capacity within a Physical Education programme. There are lots of simple tasks that are probably done without much thought; for example, looking after equipment, organising practices, offering constructive feedback or leading a warm-up activity.

physical education: beyond the curriculum

If these opportunities are being offered, it is important to make them equitable. This may mean supporting children with additional needs to be able to carry out the tasks. Furthermore, if these tasks are central to the Physical Education programme, then children and young people should know how to complete efficiently and effectively.

Making responsibility more formal, structured or explicit can help raise the status of both the role and the learning opportunities. More formal approaches may include planned programmes, such as the Sport Education initiative (see *References and Further Reading* section) or routes that lead to qualifications. For example, Sports Leaders UK has a progressive series of awards that can lead to nationally recognised qualifications. These start with the Young Leaders Award, for children aged nine, and progress through generic sports and dance leaders awards before specialising in areas of sports leadership. Governing bodies of sport also have 'access' qualifications that provide an introduction to coaching, officiating and management, many of which involve aspects of volunteering and gaining practical experience with peers and the wider community.

Other roles that can also be developed include reporters for events, marketing teams and a whole range of associated roles. Working with the learning community should open up lots of opportunities to extend the experiences of the children and young people involved.

Reflective task

- How can trained and experienced young leaders and officials support the development of opportunities detailed in *Chapters Five* to *Eight*?

- How can development opportunities be planned into these opportunities?

Lunchtime is a particularly good time to utilise young leaders as the staff available at this time often have to concentrate on priorities other than physical activity promotion. Giving young leaders activity cards that link to curriculum learning can help reinforce key points and techniques as younger children tend to be interested in what their older peers are doing.

Sports council

The concept of a school council has gained popularity over recent years. There are many benefits, including developing the school community and citizenship, giving children and young people a voice and providing a real context for social learning. Councils give children and young people responsibility for their own learning and development within a supportive framework.

Sports councils can be run in many different ways, as standalone bodies or as subcommittees of main school councils. They may be tasked with specific projects or given a free remit by the school to develop ideas. Councils may be given small budgets or be able to raise, or bid for, monies to support their plans.

Councils of this type can be very effective, but need support and training from staff and to be reminded of the limitations of their 'power'! Below are two case studies that give different ideas of how councils can work in different settings. It is important that this type of opportunity fits with existing structures within a school as some of the ideas may not be appropriate for all settings or may need to be 'phased in' over a period of time with additional training.

Case study five: A Physical Education Council in a Primary School

How the Physical Education Council operates

Two Physical Education Councils were formed within the school, one for the junior school and one for the infants. Reception and nursery children were also involved in the process, discussing issues and informing their respective council, but were not required to select representatives. Meetings were held at least once every half-term, where items were discussed and decisions made. These were reported back to class members through the elected representatives and to the full school council by the chairperson.

Why the Physical Education Council was developed

An external inspection identified two areas to improve: standards and opportunities in Physical Education; and responding to the needs of pupils. A proactive Physical Education coordinator devised a strategy that could allow the children to regain ownership of the curriculum and ensure their experiences were purposeful, enjoyable and developmental. Building on a successful school council, a subcommittee was proposed with the remit for developing Physical Education opportunities.

Student elections

Before Physical Education Council elections took place, it was agreed that the children must have an understanding of the Council's purpose and the process involved. For many of the children, particularly those who were not involved with the current school council, taking part in a democratic election would be a new experience. Class teachers explained about democratic elections, making links to governance at a national level.

The children that were interested in the concept were invited to write a letter of application against a 'job-and-skills criteria' (below), for the posts of responsibility. Letters were made anonymous and then reviewed by linked staff and the school council. Interviews took place to confirm interest, make decisions and ensure engagement. Once the interviews had taken place, two representatives from each class were chosen and a chairperson and secretary elected from within that group.

Example role outlines of duties for elected parties

The representatives should:

- take part in school Physical Education council discussions

- represent their class at council meetings

- consider the views of the pupils they represent when they make decisions

- report back to their class after school council meetings

- elect a chairperson and secretary.

Case study five (continued)

The chairperson should:

- lead meetings

- prepare the agenda for the next meeting with the help of the link teacher

- meet the head teacher to talk about any issues

- attend part of a staff or governors' meeting to report on any achievements and issues or to request help or financial support for a project

- ensure that there is a clear link between the School Council and the Physical Education Council so that the issues raised are considered to be important for the whole school and not seen as separate.

The secretary should:

- take notes during any meetings

- help prepare agendas with the link teacher and chairperson

- make sure enough copies of the minutes are sent to each class

- keep all the minutes safe in a book or file for future reference

- attend school-based adult meetings with the chairperson and take notes if necessary.

In consideration of the roles of the chairperson and secretary, it was necessary to limit the elections for these to older children.

Impact of the Physical Education Council

The impact of the Physical Education Council has been significant in encouraging involvement, raising awareness and supporting staff in developing opportunities. The Physical Education Council has worked on a range of topics, including: sports day; kit; equipment purchases; the activity environment; lessons; teaching styles used; the use of external coaches; after-school clubs; health and safety; and play provision. Once the council was fully established, its members communicated via a combination of newsletters and an online blog to pupils, teachers, parents and governors.

Case study six: Sports Council in a Girls' Secondary School

How the Sports Council operates

Students were selected on merit, based upon their commitment to developing Physical Education and school sport. These students may have also formed part of the School Council and expressed their interest in representing their views on Physical Education and school sport as part of whole-school matters. The Sports Council was also integral to the Physical Education volunteering and leadership pathway.

Why the Sports Council was developed

The need for a Sports Council came about for many reasons, some of which included: poor attendance at out-of-school-hours clubs; dissatisfaction with the Physical Education uniform; and the emergence of the School Council as a strong voice within the school. Many students wanted to volunteer time to improving Physical Education and school sport and there was also a belief among staff in the huge benefit of giving students ownership of their curriculum and out-of-school-hours learning experiences.

Student elections

At the start of every academic year, each tutor group selected a representative to take on the role of Physical Education form captain. From this, the Physical Education department elected one captain from each year to formally attend meetings. All other student representatives were also invited to attend meetings if they chose. Elected members then had the responsibility of influencing decisions on all matters relating to the student experiences of Physical Education and school sport. Sports Council meetings were held every half-term, with the Head of Sport at sixth form (or Year 11) acting as the chairperson for the meetings. An agenda was drawn from any issues that the students wished to raise on behalf of their tutor/year groups.

Impact of the Sports Council

The impact of having a Sports Council has been massive. The students view the role as a privilege and it develops positive attitudes and role models within the school. Since the introduction of the Sports Council, a new Physical Education uniform (designed and agreed by the Sports Council) has been introduced, out-of-hours programmes are now under constant review and students have complete influence over what is being delivered. The Sports Council also played a large role in developing the concept of a sports week, where students' sporting interests are represented where possible. Students from the Sports Council now take complete responsibility in communicating messages and promoting achievements within Physical Education and sport and have a regular slot within whole-school assemblies to do this. The final major impact of the Sports Council has been the hugely successful introduction of inter-school competitions and well-organised events, which would not have been possible to run without their help.

'Chinese' start to the day

In *Chapter One* it was suggested that physical activity can improve mental performance. Although there is no direct causal evidence as yet, there is some basic physiology that supports this proposal. Physical activity makes the body work harder and blood flow more readily around the body. This blood carries oxygen to all parts of the body, including the brain, which is the part of the body where thought and 'mental' activity takes place before being enacted by the rest of the body.

Not all physical activities take up a lot of space or need a lot of preparation; there are lots of programmes such as the Youth Sport Trust's 'Wake and Shake', 'Take 10' from Devonshire local authority and many variants on the yoga and aerobics approaches to movement available. Brain Gym® activities are also popular and can be done in small spaces, helping to reinvigorate the body and, therefore, the brain. Simple stretching activities, particularly if children and young people have been sitting down for a long time, can work to realign the body and release tension. If our bodies are working more effectively then, surely, we will be in a better position to learn.

Practical learning and cross-curricular links

Schools should, and in most cases do, use a wide range of pedagogical approaches, skills and techniques to enable learning for all children across the curriculum. However, learning by physically 'doing' is often underused as an approach, with many curricular lessons being classroom-based and the children and young people sat at a desk. Taking opportunities to involve movement can engage a wider number of children and act as a contrast to more formal learning.

For the purpose of this book, there are two fairly distinct ways to consider this topic. Activities that use movement as the means for learning a particular outcome or subject (ie practical learning) and activities that develop understanding of Physical Education with, or through, another subject (cross curricular). Many practitioners already use these opportunities, particularly within early-years education settings; explicitly mapping out the links can not only help evidence the effort being put into the planning process, but will also help the children and young people, who, on recognising links between different areas of the curriculum, can subsequently make connections between the different things they are learning.

Table 7: Cross-curricular links and active learning ideas

Subject Area	Physical Learning (ie learning something physically)	Cross Curricular (ie subjects supporting each other)
Art	Artistic dance	Sport and movement as a stimulus for art Art as a stimulus for movement
Citizenship	Practical leadership activities	Roles and responsibilities Careers in sport and health
English	Drama activities Story-telling Human semaphore – spelling using either body parts or whole bodies	Speaking and listening Writing reports Planning Reading instructions Technical language and terminology
Geography	Orienteering and directional language	Mapping
History	Exploration of historical venues or routes/roadways Using orienteering skills on a treasure hunt to find historical clues and artefacts	Learning dances from different cultures and historical periods Investigating the development of sport and leisure through time
ICT	Physical performances to be monitored (eg using heart rate monitors) Following directions – programmable toys	Video analysis of movement, technique and performance Global Positioning System orienteering
Mathematics	Exploring properties of shape and dimensions Counting and ordering activities	Using statistics from a sporting event for analysis Measurement of distances in athletic events Positional language
Modern Foreign Languages	Responding to movement vocabulary	Learning key words in different languages
Music	Responding to and creating rhythm	Composing music for events

Subject Area	Physical Learning (ie learning something physically)	Cross Curricular (ie subjects supporting each other)
Religious Education and Personal, social and Moral Education	Team-building and trust development	Moral dilemmas in sport and health Issues relating to religion, faith and sport
Science	Experiments relating to movement and exercise or forces	Sport science Biomechanics
Technology (including Design Technology)	Exploring bridges – human suspension bridge	Technology in sport Planning and creating

Reflective task

An alternative is to use a theme from Physical Education to form the basis of a large-scale cross-curricular project. Consider the Olympic Games and Paralympic Games; how could each subject area link to these massive events?

Lunchtime and break time

Traditionally, break time and lunchtime have offered excellent opportunities for physical play. Sadly, though, through a combination of wider pressures both within and outside of school, time for play and opportunities has, perhaps, lessened. It is also worrying that the skills children used to naturally acquire for spontaneous play have all but disappeared in the current climate of the Internet, television and computer consoles. Many of these issues are discussed in the thought-provoking book *Toxic Childhood* by Sue Palmer.

This time within the day has also often been seen as 'free time' where children and young people should be able to choose what they do. This is important, but given the vision of this book (to harness every opportunity in making physical activity central to children and young peoples' lives) this may need considering. Choice is essential, but there is no harm in offering quality opportunities for children and young people to choose from, or be guided towards.

Initially, this may mean disrupting established patterns of play so that the needs of all can be met. Often, games such as football dominate the play space, giving little opportunity for those who do not wish to take part, to play in the large areas of space. It is worth considering the benefits gained through playtime football or similar opportunities. Do these children and young people have access to this opportunity at other times? Does it fit within their training and competition schedules? Does it contribute to a broad experience of physical activity? Does it develop their physical skills or, indeed, their social skills?

This is not to say that football should be 'banned' in playgrounds, more that schools should think about limiting it to a few sessions a week so that wider opportunities can be explored. One idea that has been developed is that of 'zoning'. Essentially, this means that different areas of the play area are designated on different days for different types of activity. These may include skipping, dance, problem-solving or modified team games such as netball, football, skills circuits, traditional games and quiet areas.

When arranging zoning areas there are some key questions to consider:

- Is there a range of opportunities, including both competitive and cooperative activities?

- How can young leaders and volunteers be used?

- How can supervisors be trained to support these ideas?

It is not a case of forcing children and young people to be active during these times as these are their 'down times'. However, if curricular opportunities are inspiring them, and they have a desire to develop and be active, this should be enabled in as many ways as possible.

Working with the members of the learning community who supervise during lunch breaks is essential. They need to be valued for what they already do and respected for what they can do. They need to be empowered so training that may lead to qualifications should be offered as part of the employment. This may be generic, relating to positive-behaviour management or organising play opportunities, or more specific in terms of a basic activity-specific qualification. Break-time supervisors will have lots of experience as to what and where different 'hotspots' are during the children and young people's free time and can thus, provide additional insight into auditing, planning and monitoring programmes.

Case study seven: Activity Leaders

Activity Leaders was established to support midday supervisors in developing physical activity at lunchtime. Older children within the school were invited to attend training on how to organise activities, talk to and help younger children and manage behaviour.

The Activity Leaders could be trained in different areas such as traditional games, skipping, team challenges, small-sided sports, skills development, dance, walking or orienteering. They could also have specific training on working with very young children, peer mediation and safe practice.

The older children volunteered to work in teams on a weekly rota, although more time was offered to those who were willing. The volunteers were supported by midday supervisors and were authorised to warn children about bad behaviour.

At the end of each session each Activity Leader recorded his or her thoughts on the session within a handbook. This handbook also included ideas for games and activities.

The Activity Leaders would take an early lunch to give them time to set up and were provided with a kit to support their status. After six sessions, Activity Leaders were rewarded with a certificate and became Bronze Leaders. After 12 sessions, they rose to Silver Leader and Gold Leader status was awarded to those who led 20 sessions and received a recommendation from midday supervisors. Gold Leaders were invited back to help with training the following year. Younger children could nominate Activity Leaders for special recognition if they felt that they had been particularly helpful or kind.

Displays

One additional way to inform, communicate and celebrate learning within and beyond the curriculum is by means of a display. A creative display can ensure that information is accessible to all children and young people, at times that suit them. External displays or noticeboards can also help to engage the wider learning community.

Displays can include a whole range of information, for example:

- artwork

- celebrations

- information about national events

- information about session leaders

- local community opportunities

- newsletters

- new opportunities

- photographs

- results

- reviews

- Sports Council announcements

- timetables.

Displays should be interactive and regularly updated to show that opportunities are valued and ongoing. They should not be too 'busy' but need to be engaging enough for the whole range of children and young people who access it. Essential information may need to be translated or simplified to ensure equity of opportunity.

7.3 Conclusion

Within the school structures (ie the environment, timetable, curriculum and ethos), it is important that children and young people are encouraged and supported in a numbers of ways. Although many of the opportunities promoted above are structured, there is also a need for opportunities to be spontaneous and creative, that explore and experiment with movement and aspects of Physical Education that do not fit within the planned programme.

Communication plays a significant role in establishing opportunities such as these. The school community needs to know that children and young people will be committed to these events, otherwise the time, energy and money going into them will not be gifted. For children and young people to commit, they need to know that they have some ownership of the opportunities, and that these opportunities are sustainable and will be consistently available.

The intention is that these ideas become part of everyday school life, for both the children and young people and the staff involved. Some of the ideas will become part of the habitual physical activity while others will contribute to the appreciation of the value of Physical Education and work towards raising the status of this subject within schools.

Key questions

- How do you currently make the most of everyday opportunities?

- Why not take the children and young people for a walk every day?

- What cross-curricular links and active learning ideas do you currently use?

 References and further reading

Department for Children, Schools and Families (2008) *Working Together: Listening to the Voices and Opinions of Young People*. Crown Copyright.

Hellison, D. (2003) *Teaching Responsibility through Physical Education*. Champaign: Human Kinetics. ISBN: 978-0-736-04601-5.

Palmer, S. (2007) *Toxic Childhood: How the Modern World is Damaging Our Children and What We Can Do About It*. London: Orion. ISBN: 978-0-752-880-91-4.

Penney, D. et al. (2005) *Sport Education in Physical Education*. London: Routledge. ISBN: 978-0-415289-68-8.

Siedentop, D. et al. (2004) *Complete Guide to Sport Education*. Leeds: Human Kinetics. ISBN: 978-0-736043-80-2.

In this chapter you will find:

- reasons why special events sometimes go wrong

- ways to make sure that the 'big day' goes well

- ideas about residential experiences, sports weeks and working with visitors.

8.0 Introduction

Physical Education offers a range of unique and powerful physical and personal development opportunities. Some of these enriched learning experiences are so significant that they cannot be considered as an ongoing part of the curriculum or the extended programme. They are special and may only occur once a year, allowing appropriate time and energy to be put into their planning and for the children and young people to be appropriately prepared. Positive impact from these events can be felt the whole year round and may well be the one salient memory children and young people take from their schooling. Negative impact will also establish this legacy. The opportunities this chapter will cover are of the type that colleagues will remember in one of two ways, declaring either:

'That was a nightmare, never again!' or 'The children got so much from it; why didn't we do this before?'.

So what makes the difference between these two experiences? The children and young people may well enjoy all 'different' opportunities, regardless of any missed learning opportunities or logistical nightmares. The biggest barrier to these events being sustainable is that they haven't been organised well enough. As a result, people do not want to do them again, the learning community becomes ineffective and future special opportunities are discounted.

8.1 Possible Barriers

The three main barriers to a successful event are poor organisation, limited impact and cost. Getting these wrong can lead to events being seen as a waste of time and effort, which will limit the likelihood of the event becoming a sustainable part of a Physical Education programme.

Poor organisation

Poor organisation often comes down to a lack of time, focus and/or communication. These occur when the event or opportunity is not regarded as important by senior managers or leaders in the school. Organisers need time to plan, deliver and evaluate any project, and this time needs to be agreed at the outset with those in charge. A plan should be written with time as one of the fixed limitations on what can be achieved; allowing time for contingencies is also vital.

If a project is not valued, other priorities will begin to take over and the focus of organisers will be reduced, potentially leading to mistakes and missed opportunities. Poor focus will mean that limited time is wasted or spent doing things with insufficient impact on the plan or intended outcomes. Where time is short, and focus transient, communication is likely to be ineffective. This focus on effective communication will be picked up later in this chapter, but it needs to be recognised as one of the most important factors in any successful 'special' opportunity. Without effective communication, teams from the learning community cannot function productively and plans cannot be carried out, monitored or evaluated. Poor communication can change what should be an 'annual highlight' into a 'never again'.

Limited impact

This is not to suggest that any organised special opportunity has no impact, more that the impact may not be measured well enough for it to be communicated or celebrated in any meaningful and effective way. *Chapter Four* sets out some key principles that should be considered when monitoring and evaluating impact. The biggest, most common mistake people make is not thinking about impact when planning the opportunity. Impact is when outcomes are achieved; to make events sustainable and positive, the planned outcomes need to be achieved and those involved in planning need to know that their efforts have been worthwhile. Children and young people will know their own outcomes from the opportunity, but sharing the wider learning can give context to their own experience and a chance to reflect on different experiences.

Cost implications

Great ideas often do not become a reality if no investment is made. This investment may be in terms of staff time or energy and is also likely to involve some financial investment. If money is a barrier to the event, this problem needs to be looked at creatively. It is also the reason planning and impact are so important.

Think of the event as a business opportunity. The outcome is not necessarily to make money (although this may be an element), but to enhance the opportunities for the children and young people involved. No one will invest in a business or project unless it can be shown clearly what is being aimed for and how this can be achieved. Investors will also want to know what the planned impact will be.

It is not suggested that a bank loan is the answer, but head teachers, local businesses and PTA treasurers will all have the same outlook. What is being proposed? Why is it worth doing? How will it be done? How much will it cost? What do we get out of it? These questions are is not intended to make funders look miserly or cold hearted; they should be credited for asking the right questions. If the answers are already prepared, it is more likely that funding can be secured.

8.2 Potential Solutions

Physical Education, with its inherent links to sport, dance, health and life in general, offers a myriad of possibilities for learning and activity. The philosophy of this book is that opportunities should build on the curriculum so that skills can be developed to support access to, and success in, these activities. It means that specialised language and terminology can be learnt and understood and expectations of behaviour and effort can be established and explained. Without this link and foundation, there is a danger that a special event will be seen merely as something that is just 'special'; a 'one-off' with little sustainable impact or relevance beyond the day. With all the effort that goes into the planning, preparation and delivery, schools should be aiming higher.

Table 8: Guidelines for planning and delivering a special opportunity

Before	During	After
• Plan A, B, C and your back-up plan; plan for flexibility and adaptability	• Communicate – keep communication channels open	• Debrief – what went well, what did not go well and why?
• Agree everything that needs agreeing with everyone that needs to agree	• Conviction – believe that the plan and the team will work, the time for second thoughts has passed – new ideas can wait for next year	• Evaluate, review and reflect on what the debrief shows
• Communicate (very clearly) everything that is important to everyone who needs to know.	• Flexibility – stick to your plan, but adapt where necessary	• Communicate, celebrate and use the impact as evidence
	• Track progress – how close are you to schedule? Is everything going as planned?	
	• Enjoy – it's not just for the spectators and children and young people – if people see you enjoying yourself, they will not panic that something might go wrong!	

Residential experiences

Residential experiences can, potentially, offer children and young people unique opportunities for personal development. Participants are away from home; they have to look after themselves and their belongings and manage their own time and energy with a different kind of support from the staff who attend with them. These experiences may include a sports tour, an outward-bound week, a weekend hike or a team-building day. Physical activity may play a central part or may be something that forms an important aspect or element of the experience. Whatever the opportunity, similar principles apply.

By planning a residential experience, you are planning an opportunity with huge potential for personal development and setting challenges. You are also planning something that allows for more risk and these need to be managed in a structured and appropriate manner, keeping in mind that these increased risks are part of what makes this type of opportunity worthwhile.

The biggest difference is obviously the environment in which the opportunity takes place, but a different venue should not necessarily mean different expectations on the participants or the providers.

Reflective task

Consider a climbing activity within a residential experience.

Climbing offers children and young people excellent opportunities for physical and skill development and can contribute to a healthy, active lifestyle. There are also personal and social benefits that can be gained as well as those relating to managing risk, planning and responding to problems. How can these opportunities be maximised?

In preparing for such experiences it is important that the leader from the school and the children or young people know and understand specific points.

From a leader's perspective:

- Have the children and young people any experience of climbing or any of the skills, attributes or understanding (such as language) that they will need?

- Have you worked with the climbing centre before?

- Are the staff suitably qualified and experienced to work with your group (although these are often the qualifications that are checked most rigorously, experience with the type of children you have can often be most telling)?

- How mature are the children (age is often not a good predictor of this)?

- Are there children with specific additional needs that the centre has no experience of working with?

- How do the children respond to risk and challenge?

The answers to these questions need to be picked up in preparatory meetings between staff from the school and staff from the centre. The outcomes need to be communicated to the children and young people so that they can consider the following areas:

- What do they need to know and understand to be prepared for the activity?

- What skills can they practice (and where) that may provide them with a preliminary experience and opportunity for progression of the skill?

- Do the children and young people know how they respond to challenge, risk and, in this case, working at a height?

- How can they support their friends in this activity and how will they be able to access support?

- What are the expectations of them, in terms of behaviour, effort and achievement?

This all takes time, but the additional time taken to carry out 'pre-visits' and risk assessments should be seen as an integral part of the experience and factored into any schedule being proposed. Residential experiences are time-consuming, but without the time being spent, the experience will not be as valuable as it could be. Many sites and venues for residential experiences offer pre-written risk assessments; although these can be useful, they are often generic to the centre and would need to be updated and adapted in light of the unique interaction this group will have with the venue. The assessment should take into account additional needs within the group, experience of the particular staff attending from both school and centre, as well as other factors, such as weather, time of year and time of the academic year.

Planning time for 'down time' (and sleep) is vital when scheduling any residential experience. This is important for both the sanity and safety of the children and young people and the staff! These periods of time may need the most planning, as they are the most vital. Boundaries of acceptable behaviour should be enforced strictly; otherwise the experience can be ruined for everybody rather than for just the one child or young person who is sent home.

Sports days

Although sports days have been discussed within *Chapter Six*, the organisation of such events should be based around the principles discussed within this chapter. It is vital that a sports day has a clear and communicated purpose; if participants and the 'audience' are expecting an event where competition and excellence are being tested, and this can be justified, then children and young people should be competing against others of their own ability level. This makes the competition fair and enables expectations to be set appropriately. Similarly, if the event is based on a philosophy of inclusion, setting activities or tasks that some children have no possibility of achieving does not meet the aim.

External sporting events

The media always seems to be full of images of forthcoming major sporting events. It sometimes appears that what used to be a definite seasonal rotation of sports has become a globalised, international, year-round feast. There always seems to be a World Championship or series of qualifiers. This could be seen as 'downgrading' or devaluing major events; however, if events are chosen selectively and for a definite link with work going on in school, they can be an effective stimulus for learning and activity.

It would be an interesting study to see how participation in tennis goes up during the All England Lawn Tennis Club Championships at Wimbledon or perhaps the number of young people who spend lunch breaks playing football during a World Cup. Certainly anecdotal evidence credits the Rugby World Cup victory for England in 2003 for an upturn in participation in youth rugby. Equally, the rise in popularity of ballroom and Latin dancing has certainly coincided with the successful television series 'Strictly Come Dancing'.

The events could be local, regional, national or international or they may be something that the children and young people are interested or involved in, either as participants, volunteers or spectators.

Opportunities could include:

- analysing performances

- celebrating results

- designing marketing materials for the event

- handling data and statistics

- links to opening ceremonies or cultural events

- making links to intra-school competitions and events

- skills sessions linked to the event

- visits to sites or stadia

- watching matches.

There is also the possibility of arranging for people involved in the event – from performers to officials to organisers – to come and visit the children or young people in the school.

Working with visitors

As children and young people grow and mature, they make more and more sense of their world from the links they make outside of their immediate families; for example, from friends' families or teachers and the wider community. With the right support and preparation, these links can be used effectively to enhance learning.

These external interactions could be in a number of forms. Visitors taking part in assemblies (see *Chapter Seven*) or work with year groups can hit a larger audience, but smaller interview groups or target group sessions may give more impact. The key is to make the sessions as focused as possible; the visitors will welcome information about the groups, what is expected and also where their contribution fits into the bigger picture. They may also want to know what outcomes you hope will result from the session. The children and young people should also come prepared to these sessions, hence getting the most out of them. Have they read or researched about the person or organisation? Can they formulate questions or stimulate debate?

Try to make it more than just a story about what the person has achieved or is aiming to do. These are often people who have overcome barriers to their participation and have shown great commitment to reach their goals. Children and young people should leave these sessions feeling positive about what they have heard, perhaps aspiring to participate in that activity, but more importantly, having learnt something about how they can better their own lives.

It is also important to consider follow-up opportunities from visitors attending sessions. Can the children and young people go to their linked community club or watch them on television? Is there some way that they can support ongoing developments?

It is essential these visits are well planned and focus on impact. Preparing for the visit is vital, but being able to articulate what impact it has had is also important. It is not about having many visitors, but ensuring that they, and the children and young people, get the most they can from the experience. Carefully vetting potential visitors is essential, both in terms of child protection and suitability of content, so working with local schools and clubs to set up a network of contacts can be useful.

Sponsored events

Schools often hold events to raise money for particular causes, which may be internal (ie building work or resources) or external (ie local, national or international causes). As with any event, what is the purpose? Is it just to raise money? How does the charity link to the event that is being held?

Often the sponsored event will have a link to Physical Education. It may be a tournament, an endurance event or a festival with some sports-related activities. It is important that these are seen as contributing to the overall 'offer' of Physical Education and the activities should support the ethos of the charity being supported and the ethos of the school in relation to Physical Education.

Time can be spent learning about the charity for which money is being raised. For example, if the school is holding a sports event in aid of a local blind support centre, help the children and young people to understand the difficulties people with visual impairment may have when participating in these activities themselves? Find out if the funding would go towards developing opportunities for physical activity.

Health or sports week

It is possible that all of the above ideas and those shared within *Chapters Five, Six* and *Seven* seem appealing and worthy of a try. One way that several ideas can be used at once (and some impetus can be gained for the school as a whole) is through a 'sports' or 'health' week. This is where a week, or part thereof, of the curriculum is given over to a series of events that can extend, enrich or enhance the usual provision. Although this is within curriculum time, the nature of this opportunity means that it is classed as a 'special opportunity' and 'beyond the curriculum'. If nothing else, it would be a little tiring if the curriculum was only this.

 Ideas 1: Example Timetable of a Sports Week in a Primary School

There are three types of opportunity that should be considered when planning an event such as this, which may be drawn from everyday, special, competitive or out-of-school-hours provision, but should also link to the curriculum:

- **Showcase** opportunities demonstrate what is already happening within the school and local community. These should be established activities that children and young people have already accessed and learnt. They may include competitions based on curricular learning, demonstrations of learning from extended opportunities or training opportunities for young leaders.

- **Preview** events highlight opportunities that are planned for the future. For example, it may be a new activity to be run in a club, new equipment for playtime or a new club that is being set up in the local community.

- **Treats** are activities that perhaps are not feasible to have as sustainable opportunities within the school programme, but can act as a stimulus for engagement. They may include visits from local sports stars, health-and-fitness testing from the local primary care trust or a sponsored event.

Before a programme is put together, questions need to be considered in relation to **aims, planning and the learning community**.

Table 9: Questions to consider when planning a sports or health week opportunity

Aims	Planning	Learning Community
• What are you trying to achieve from the 'week'? • What learning are you targeting from the experience? • What are some of the things that you would really like to be able to do?	• How much time do you have? • Has the whole week been waivered or are other lessons still going to continue? • How long do you have to prepare? • When is the best time to run this event? Will it clash with preparation for other events or priorities? • When will you be able to communicate the plan to everyone involved? • How will you launch and close the week? • What preparatory learning and tasks need to be done with the children and young people?	• Who else is involved? • How is school management involved and supporting the project? • Are you being asked to prepare everything or will all staff be preparing aspects of the event? • What links do you have within the local community? • How can you use the children and young people? • How will the Sports Council and Young Leaders be involved? • What is your role? • Which local media outlets can be involved? • How will you keep everyone informed and involved? • How can you ensure quality of outside providers? • Who is in charge of considering issues of equality, safety, risk assessment, child protection and first aid?

It is imperative that everyone involved signs up to the plan and the programme, and commits themselves to the required roles and responsibilities.

physical education: beyond the curriculum

8.3 Conclusion

All special opportunities have the potential to go wrong, which is why the principles surrounding preparation, purpose and impact are critical to any success. Taking the time to persuade school leaders and managers about the potential impact of the events is central to the process. Using the time allowed to create, implement and evaluate the event is also a significant factor. Start small and gradually build up the repertoire of events and opportunities the programme delivers.

Key questions

* Why is there a need for special opportunities beyond your curriculum provision?

* What makes your current 'special events' special?

* How do your special events contribute to the broader learning experience of the children and young people?

 References and further reading

Whitlam, P. and Beaumont, G. (2008) *Safe Practice in Physical Education and School Sport*. Leeds: Coachwise Business Solutions. ISBN: 978-1-905540-54-9.

education: beyond the curriculum

Final Thoughts

This book has aimed to justify why schools should look to extend their Physical Education programmes 'beyond the curriculum'. It has also looked to challenge practice and provide ideas as to what can be done to extend the existing programme. These need to be linked to curriculum provision, so that all children and young people can progress through the opportunities and make the most of what is on offer.

We do not suggest that one person can do all of this for the school. It is essential that the whole school and local community are involved, building on the school's ethos. If a school could sustain all the opportunities outlined in this book, there is no doubt that children and young people would have access to an immense array of opportunities to develop their physical education, health and wellbeing. However, this would not guarantee they would reach their sporting potential, maintain peak fitness and health or even participate in physical activity throughout their lifetime as, unfortunately, life is never that simple and too many variables are involved.

The opportunities outlined in this book need to be organised and managed in a way that focuses on the needs of all children and young people and their aspirations and dreams. All involved must have children and young people at the centre of the programme, rather than a list of activities they can run or arrange. This would provide an opportunity for all children and young people to develop the foundations necessary to make the best possible progress towards a healthy, active lifestyle by developing the skills, understanding, attitude, confidence and motivation to take part.

Action planning

Now is the time to plan the next steps by identifying what you wish to change or implement.

List	Action	Why?	By When?	Ranking of Importance
1				
2				
3				
4				
5				

Next:

Action	Where are You Now?	Where Would You Like to Be?	What is Required?

physical education: beyond the curriculum

Frequently Asked Questions (FAQs)

Thank you to all the colleagues, course delegates and especially the students at Roehampton University who have provided this almost endless list of questions about Physical Education beyond the curriculum. At least they are interested!

The page references below relate to where, in the resource, each topic is discussed.

Working with Sports Coaches

- How can you find and keep a good coach? (page 18)

- What qualifications do coaches need? (page 19)

- What type of experience should a coach have? (page 19)

- What do you need to check when employing a coach? (pages 19–21)

- Who can I talk to about finding a coach? (page 21)

- What information will a coach need to know about my class? (page 21)

- Who is responsible if things go wrong? (page 22)

- What can I do if I have a complaint? (page 22)

- What standards should I expect? (page 22)

- How can I involve parents effectively in extended programmes? (page 24)

- Do I, or the sports coach, need to keep registers? (page 42)

- Should children pay for clubs? (page 54)

- Should a club be run all year round? (page 54)

Wider Questions

physical education: beyond the curriculum

Bibliography

Andrews, C. (2005) *Meeting SEN in the Curriculum: PE/Sports*. London: David Fulton Publishers. ISBN: 978-1-843121-64-0.

Arnold, P. J. (1979) *Meaning in Movement, Sport and Physical Education*. London: Heinemann Educational Publishers. ISBN: 978-0-435800-33-8.

Association for Physical Education and sports coach UK (2007) *Adults Supporting Learning (including Coaches and Volunteers): A framework for development*. Leeds: Coachwise Business Solutions. ISBN: 978-1-905540-28-0.

Association for Physical Education (2008a) 'Health Position Paper: Physical Education and its contribution to public health', *Physical Education Matters*, 3 (2): 8–12.

Association for Physical Education (2008b) 'Manifesto for a World-class System for Physical Education', *Physical Education Matters*, 3 (4): 31–32.

Auweele, Y. V. and Biddle, S. (eds) *Psychology for Physical Educators*. Leeds: Human Kinetics Europe Ltd. ISBN: 978-0-736062-40-4.

BAALPE, CCPR, PEA UK, PE ITT Network (2005) Declaration from the National Summit for Physical Education: London, 24 January 2005', www.afpe.org.uk/public/downloads/national_summit.pdf

Bailey, R. (2001) *Teaching Physical Education: A Handbook for Primary and Secondary School Teachers*. Abingdon: Routledge. ISBN: 978-0-749434-46-5.

Bailey, R., Armour, K., Kirk, D., Jess, M., Pickup, I. and Sandford, R. (2008) 'The Educational Benefits Claimed for Physical Education and School Sport: An Academic Review.' *Research Papers in Education*, 24 (1): 1–27.

Bell, J. (2005) *Doing Your Research Project*. Buckingham: Open University Press. ISBN: 978-0-335215-04-1.

Coates, J. and Vickerman, P. (2008) 'Let the children have their say: a review of children with special educational needs and their experiences of Physical Education', *British Journal of Learning Support*, 23 (4): 168–175.

Cohen, L., Manion, L. and Morrison, K. (2008) *Research Methods in Education*. London: Routledge ISBN: 978-0-415368-78-0.

Creswell, J. (2008) *Research Design Qualitative, Quantitative and Mixed Methods Approaches*. London: Sage. ISBN: 978-1-412965-57-6.

David, T. (1994) *Working Together for Young People: Multi-professionalism in Action*. London: Routledge. ISBN: 978-0-415092-48-7.

Deci, E. L. and Ryan, R.N. (1985) *Intrinsic Motivation and Self-determination in Human Behavior*. London: Plenum Press. ISBN: 978-0-306420-22-1.

Department for Children, Schools and Families (2008) *Working Together: Listening to the Voices and Opinions of Young People*. Crown Copyright.

Doherty, J. and Brennan, P. (2008) *Physical Education and Development 3–11: A Guide for Teachers*. Abingdon: David Fulton Publishers. ISBN: 978-1-843124-56-6.

Drewe, S. B. (1998) 'Competing Conceptions of Competition: Implications for Physical Education', *European Physical Education Review*, 4 (1): 5–20.

Evans, J., Rich, E. and Davies, B. (2008) ''Health Education or Weight Management in Schools?', *Physical Education Matters*, 3 (1): 28–32

Gallahue, D. L. and Ozmun, J. C. (2006) *Understanding Motor Development: Infants, Children, Adolescents, Adults*. London: McGraw-Hill Higher Education Publishers. ISBN: 978- 0-071244-44-2.

Green, K. (2000) 'Extra-Curricular Physical Education in England and Wales: A Sociological Perspective on a Sporting Bias', *Physical Education and Sport Pedagogy*. 5(2): 179–207.

Green, K. (2004) 'Physical Education, lifelong participation and "the couch potato society"', *Physical Education and Sport Pedagogy*, 9(1): 73–85.

Green, K. (2008) *Understanding Physical Education*. London: Sage Ltd. ISBN: 978-1-412921-13-8.

Griggs, G. (2007a) 'Looking on from the sidelines: Inclusion in Primary Physical Education', *Physical Education Matters*, 2(1): vii.

Griggs, G. (2007b) 'Physical Education: Primary Matters, Secondary Importance', *Education 3–13: International Journal of Primary, Elementary and Early Years Education*. 35 (1): 59–69.

Haydn-Davies, D., Pickup, I. and Jess, M. (2007) 'The Challenges and Potential within Primary Physical Education', *Physical Education Matters*, 2 (1): 12–15.

Hayes, S. and Stidder, G. (2003) *Equity and Inclusion in Physical Education and Sport*. London: Routledge. ISBN: 978-0-415282-26-0.

Hellison, D. (2003) *Teaching Responsibility through Physical Education*. Champaign: Human Kinetics. ISBN: 978-0-736-04601-5.

Kay, W. (2002) 'Physical Education R.I.P?', *British Journal of Teaching Physical Education*, 34 (4): 6–10.

Kirk, D. (2005) 'Physical Education, Youth sport and lifelong participation: the importance of the early learning experiences', *European Physical Education Review*, 11 (3): 239–255.

Kirk, D. and Gorely, T. (2000) 'Challenging Thinking About the Relationship Between School Physical Education and Sport Performance', *European Physical Education Review*, 6 (2): 119–134.

Lee, M. J. (2003) 'Values in Physical Education and Sport: a conflict of interests?' *British Journal of Teaching Physical Education*, 35 (1): 6–10.

McNamee, M. (2005) 'The Nature and Values of Physical Education', in Green, K. and Hardman, K. (eds) *Physical Education: Essential Issues*. London: Sage Publications Ltd. ISBN: 978-1-761944-98-0.

Morley, D. Bailey, R. Tan, J. and Cooke, B. (2005) 'Inclusive Physical Education: teachers' views of including pupils with Special Educational Needs and/or disabilities in Physical Education', *European Physical Education Review*, 11(1): 84–107.